MILITARY HISTORY
FROM PRIMARY SOURCES

MEDIEVAL WARFARE

JAMES GRANT

EDITED AND INTRODUCED
BY BOB CARRUTHERS

Pen & Sword
MILITARY

This edition published in 2013 by
Pen & Sword Military
An imprint of
Pen & Sword Books Ltd
47 Church Street
Barnsley
South Yorkshire
S70 2AS

First published in Great Britain in 2012 in digital format by
Coda Books Ltd.

Copyright © Coda Books Ltd, 2012
Published under licence by Pen & Sword Books Ltd.

ISBN 978 1 78159 224 3

This book contains an extract from 'British Battles on Land and Sea' by James
Grant. Published by Cassell and Company Limited, 1894.

A CIP catalogue record for this book is
available from the British Library

Printed and bound by
CPI Group (UK) Ltd, Croydon, CR0 4YY

Pen & Sword Books Ltd incorporates the Imprints of Pen & Sword Aviation, Pen
& Sword Family History, Pen & Sword Maritime, Pen & Sword Military, Pen
& Sword Discovery, Pen & Sword Politics, Pen & Sword Atlas, Pen & Sword
Archaeology, Wharncliffe Local History, Wharncliffe True Crime, Wharncliffe
Transport, Pen & Sword Select, Pen & Sword Military Classics, Leo Cooper, The
Praetorian Press, Claymore Press, Remember When, Seaforth Publishing and
Frontline Publishing

For a complete list of Pen & Sword titles please contact
PEN & SWORD BOOKS LIMITED
47 Church Street, Barnsley, South Yorkshire, S70 2AS, England
E-mail: enquiries@pen-and-sword.co.uk
Website: www.pen-and-sword.co.uk

CONTENTS

AN INTRODUCTION TO MEDIEVAL WARFARE

THE EXPERIENCE level and tactical manoeuvring ability of medieval armies varied depending on the period and region. For larger battles, pre-battle planning typically consisted of a council of the war leaders, which could either be the general laying down a plan or a noisy debate between the different leaders, depending on how much authority the general possessed. Battlefield communications before the advent of strict lines of communication were naturally very difficult. Communication was done through musical signals, audible commands, messengers, or visual signals such as raising a standard banner or flag.

The infantry, including missile troops (such as archers), would typically be employed at the outset of the battle to break open infantry formations while the cavalry attempted to defeat its opposing number. If the cavalry met foot soldiers, the pikemen would engage them. Perhaps the most important technological advancement for medieval warfare in Europe was the invention of the stirrup. It most likely came to Europe with the Avars in the 7th century, although it was not properly adopted by the major European powers until the 10th century.

Once one side coaxed their opposing infantry into breaking formation, the cavalry would be deployed in attempt to exploit the loss of cohesion in the opposing infantry lines and begin slaying the infantrymen in the pandemonium. Once a break in the lines was exploited, the cavalry became instrumental to victory, causing further breakage in the lines and wreaking havoc amongst the infantrymen, as it is much easier to kill a man from the top of a horse than to stand on the ground and face a half-ton destrier (large warhorse) carrying an armed knight. However, until a significant break in the enemy infantry lines arose, the cavalry could not be used to much effect against infantry since horses are not easily harried into a wall of pikemen. Pure infantry conflicts would be lengthy and drawn-out.

Muzzle-loaded cannons were introduced to the battlefield in the later medieval period. However, their very poor rate of fire (which often meant that only one shot was fired in the course of an entire battle) and their inaccuracy made them more of a psychological force multiplier than an effective anti-personnel weapon. Later on in medieval warfare, once hand cannons were introduced, the rate of fire improved only slightly, but the cannons became far easier to aim, largely because they were smaller and much closer to their wielder. Their users could be easily protected, because the cannons were lighter and could be moved far more quickly.

A hasty retreat could cause greater casualties than an organized withdrawal, because the fast cavalry of the winning side's rearguard would intercept the fleeing enemy while their infantry continued their attack. In most medieval battles, more soldiers were killed during the retreat than in battle, since mounted knights could quickly and easily dispatch the archers and infantry who were no longer protected by a line of pikes as they had been during the previous fighting.

FORTIFICATIONS

Breakdowns in centralized states led to the rise of a number of groups that turned to large-scale pillage as a source of income. Most notably the Vikings (but also Arabs, Mongols and Magyars) raided significantly. As these groups were generally small and needed to move quickly, building fortifications was a good way to provide refuge and protection for the people and the wealth in the region.

These fortifications evolved over the course of the Middle Ages, the most important form being the castle, a structure which has become linked with the medieval era to many. The castle served as a protected place for the local elites. Inside a castle they were protected from bands of raiders and could send mounted warriors to drive the raiders from the area, or to disrupt the efforts of larger armies to supply themselves in the region by gaining local superiority over foraging parties that would be impossible against the whole enemy host.

Fortifications were a very important part of warfare because they provided safety to the lord, his family, and his servants. They provided refuge from armies too large to face in open battle. The ability of the heavy cavalry to dominate a battle on an open field was useless against fortifications. Building siege engines was a time-consuming process, and could seldom be effectively done without preparations before the campaign. Many sieges could take months, if not years, to weaken or demoralize the defenders sufficiently. Fortifications were an excellent means of ensuring that the elite could not be easily dislodged from their lands - as Count Baldwin of Hainaut commented in 1184 on seeing enemy troops ravage his lands from the safety of his castle, "they can't take the land with them".

SIEGE WARFARE

In the Medieval period besieging armies used a wide variety of siege engines including: scaling ladders; battering rams; siege towers and various types of catapults such as the mangonel, onager, ballista, and trebuchet. Siege techniques also included mining in which tunnels were dug under a section of the wall and then rapidly collapsed to destabilize the wall's foundation. A final technique was to bore into the enemy walls, however this was not nearly as effective as other methods due to the thickness of castle walls. Several of these siege techniques were used by the Romans but experienced a rebirth during the Crusades.

The Walls of Dubrovnik are a series of defensive stone walls, never breached by hostile army, that have surrounded and protected a maritime city-state of Dubrovnik (Ragusa), situated in southern Croatia.

Advances in the prosecution of sieges encouraged the development of a variety of defensive counter-measures. In particular, medieval fortifications became progressively stronger - for example, the advent of the concentric castle from the period of the Crusades - and more dangerous to attackers - witness the increasing use of machicolations and murder-holes, as well the preparation of hot or incendiary substances. Arrow slits, concealed doors for sallies, and deep water wells were also integral to resisting siege at this time. Designers of castles paid particular attention to defending entrances, protecting gates with drawbridges, portcullises and barbicans. Wet animal skins were often draped over gates to repel fire. Moats and other water defenses, whether natural or augmented, were also vital to defenders.

In the Middle Ages, virtually all large cities had city walls - Dubrovnik in Dalmatia is an impressive and well-preserved example - and more important cities had citadels, forts or castles. Great effort was expended to ensure a good water supply inside the city in case of siege. In some cases, long tunnels were constructed to carry water into the city. In other cases, such as the Ottoman siege of Shkodra, Venetian engineers had designed and installed cisterns that were fed by rain water channeled by a system of conduits in the walls and buildings. Complex systems of underground tunnels were used for storage and communications in medieval cities like Tábor in Bohemia. Against these would be matched the mining skills of teams of trained sappers, who were sometimes employed by besieging armies.

Until the invention of gunpowder-based weapons (and the resulting higher-velocity projectiles), the balance of power and logistics definitely favored the defender. With the invention of gunpowder, the traditional methods of defense became less and less effective against a determined siege.

ORGANIZATION

The medieval knight was usually a mounted and armoured soldier, often connected with nobility or royalty, although (especially in north-eastern Europe) knights could also come from the lower classes, and could even be unfree persons. The cost of their armor, horses, and weapons was great; this, among other things, helped gradually transform the knight, at least in western Europe, into a distinct social class separate from other warriors. During the crusades, holy orders of Knights fought in the Holy Land (see Knights Templar, the Hospitallers, etc.).

Heavily armed cavalry, armed with lances and a varied assortment of hand weapons played a significant part in the battles of the Middle Ages. The heavy cavalry consisted of wealthy knights and noblemen who could afford the equipment and non-noble squires employed by noblemen. Heavy cavalry was the difference between victory and defeat in many key battles. Their thunderous charges could break the lines of most infantry formations, making them a valuable asset to all medieval armies.

Hungarian raids in the 10th century. Most European nations were praying for mercy: "Sagittis hungarorum libera nos Domine" - "Lord save us from the arrows of Hungarians."

Light cavalry consisted usually of lighter armed and armoured men, who could have lances, javelins or missile weapons, such as bows or crossbows. In the Dark Ages and much of the Middle Ages light cavalry usually consisted of wealthy commoners.

Later in the Middle Ages light cavalry would also include sergeants who were men who had trained as knights but could not afford the costs associated with the title. Light cavalry were used as scouts, skirmishers or outflankers. Many countries developed their own styles of light cavalry, such as Hungarian mounted archers, Spanish jinetes, Italian and German mounted crossbowmen and English currours.

Costumes of Roman and German Soldiers From Miniatures on different Manuscripts, from the Sixth to the Twelfth Centuries. Infantry were recruited and trained in a wide variety of manners in different regions of Europe all through the Middle Ages, and probably always formed the most numerous part of a medieval field army. Many infantrymen in prolonged wars would be mercenaries. Most armies contained significant numbers of spearmen, archers and other unmounted soldiers. In sieges, perhaps the most common element of medieval warfare,[citation needed] infantry units served as garrison troops and archers, among other positions. Near the end of the Middle Ages, with the advancements of weapons and armour, the infantryman became more important to an army.

RECRUITING

In the earliest Middle Ages it was the obligation of every noble to respond to the call to battle with his own equipment, archers, and infantry. This decentralized system was necessary due to the social order of the time, but could lead to motley forces with variable training, equipment and abilities. The more resources the noble had access to, the better his troops would typically be. Typically the feudal armies consisted of a core of highly skilled knights and their household troops, mercenaries hired for the time of the campaign and feudal levies fulfilling their feudal obligations, who usually were little more than rabble.

They could, however, be efficient in disadvantageous terrain. Towns and cities could also field militias.

As central governments grew in power, a return to the citizen and mercenary armies of the classical period also began, as central levies of the peasantry began to be the central recruiting tool. It was estimated that the best infantrymen came from the younger sons of free land-owning yeomen, such as the English archers and Swiss pikemen. England was one of the most centralized states in the Late Middle Ages, and the armies that fought the Hundred Years' War were mostly paid professionals. In theory, every Englishman had an obligation to serve for forty days. Forty days was not long enough for a campaign, especially one on the continent. Thus the scutage was introduced, whereby most Englishmen paid to escape their service and this money was used to create a permanent army. However, almost all high medieval armies in Europe were composed of a great deal of paid core troops, and there was a large mercenary market in Europe from at least the early 12th century.

As the Middle Ages progressed in Italy, Italian cities began to rely mostly on mercenaries to do their fighting rather than the militias that had dominated the early and high medieval period in this region. These would be groups of career soldiers who would be paid a set rate. Mercenaries tended to be effective soldiers, especially in combination with standing forces, but in Italy they came to dominate the armies of the city states. This made them problematic; while at war they were considerably more reliable than a standing army, at peacetime they proved a risk to the state itself like the Praetorian Guard had once been. Mercenary-on-mercenary warfare in Italy led to relatively bloodless campaigns which relied as much on manoeuvre as on battles, since the condottieri recognized it was more efficient to attack the enemy's ability to wage war rather than his battle forces, discovering the concept of indirect warfare 500 years before Sir Basil Liddell Hart, and attempting to attack the enemy supply lines, his economy and his ability to wage war rather than risking an open battle, and manoeuvre him into a position where risking a battle would have been suicidal. Macchiavelli misunderstood the indirect approach as cowardice.

The knights were drawn to battle by feudal and social obligation, and also by the prospect of profit and advancement. Those who performed well were likely to increase their landholdings and advance in the social hierarchy. The prospect of significant income from pillage and ransoming prisoners was also important. For the mounted knight Medieval Warfare could be a relatively low risk affair. Nobles avoided killing each other, rather preferring capturing them alive, for several reasons - for one thing, many were related to each other, had fought alongside one another, and they were all (more or less) members of the same elite culture; for another, a noble's ransom could be very high, and indeed some made a living by capturing and ransoming nobles in battle. Even peasants, who did not share the bonds of kinship and culture, would often avoid killing a nobleman, valuing the high ransom that a live capture could bring, as well as the valuable horse, armour and equipment that came with him. However, this is by no means a rule of medieval warfare. It was quite common, even at the height of "chivalric" warfare, for the knights to suffer heavy casualties during battles.

- C H A P T E R   I -
HASTINGS, 1066

THE MOST important battle ever fought on English soil is unquestionably that of Hastings; not only because of the great strength of the invading force, the perfect success of the enterprise, and the dreadful misery which fell upon the conquered English for several generations, till the Norman element became blended, if not altogether lost, in the Saxon, but also on account of many incidents peculiar to that short and terrible war.

From the day of the accession of Harold, the son of Godwin, to the English throne, the dread of a Norman invasion haunted him, for William of Normandy had sworn to stake on the issue of battle his personal right to that throne, which he claimed as the bequest of the Confessor; and during the summer of 1066 all his dukedom and the territories of his adherents resounded with the notes of preparation. He received a banner, consecrated by the Pope; and through all Maine and Anjou, Poitou and Bretagne, Flanders, Aquitaine, and Burgundy, the mail was burnished, the spear flashed, and the steed galloped; while lawless barons, whose ruined castles now stud the Rhine, wild robbers from the base of the Alps, knight, varlet, and vagrant, we are told, all mustered to join this holy banner, that was to be the guide to the pillage and conquest of England.

"Good pay and broad lands to every one who will serve Duke William with spear, with sword, and bow," was said on all hands; and the duke himself added to Fitz-Osborn, as in perspective he parcelled out the fair land of England in fiefs to his Norman knights, "This Harold hath not the strength of mind to promise the least of those things that belong to me. But I have the right to promise that which is mine, and also that which belongs to him. He must be the victor who can give away both his own and that which belongs to the foe."

The Normans were then in the zenith of their military glory. In France they had acquired a noble territory; a few of their adventurous knights, by overcoming Italians, Greeks, and Germans, had laid the foundation of the opulent kingdom of Naples and Sicily: and thus the friends of William were as confident of success as they were resolute and fearless.

Every harbour and roadstead in his dominions and in those of his allies was busy with preparation throughout the summer and spring of that eventful year. Workmen were employed at all the ports, building ships, setting up masts, and stretching sails. William had need of ships to cope with that Saxon navy which was the legacy of Alfred; for now "the last of the Saxon kings" had assembled at Sandwich the largest fleet and army that England had ever seen, to resist the coming invaders, though the population was not then supposed to exceed 2,000,000, while two of the present English border counties, Westmoreland and Cumberland, belonged to the King of Scotland.

Thierry estimates the entire fleet of William as amounting to 400 ships with masts and sails, and more than 1,000 transport boats (Hume says 3,000 sail); while his army, now fully collected, was carefully organised by him according to the tactics of the day, and its fiery masses were welded together by the powerful and combined influences of love of glory and adventure, fanaticism, conquest, and plunder.

They mustered 60,000 men. Among them were Eustace, Count of Boulogne, Ameri de Thouars, Hugh d'Etaples, Guillaume d'Evreux, Geoffrey de Rotau, Roger de Beaumont, Guillaume de Warrenne, Roger de Montgomerie, Hugh de Grantmesnil, Charles Martel, and other knights and nobles, whose muster-roll of names, as given by Grafton, in his "Black Letter Chronicle," published in 1572, amounts to 753. Among them was René, a monk of Fécamp, who substituted a shirt of mail for his cassock, to follow William with a ship and twenty men-at-arms, on receiving the promise of an English bishopric. The rendezvous was the mouth .of the Dive, between the Seine and the Orme, and thence the armament was to sail in the middle of August. Sir Robert le Blount, styled "Dux Navium Militarium," was commander of the fleet.

North-west winds delayed William till the beginning of September. Ere this the Saxon fleet at Sandwich had melted away, being unprovisioned. Just at the time, too, when Harold's presence was all-important on the south coast, he was called northwards to repel a Norwegian army that had landed under the banner of Harold Hardrada, the last of the Scandinavian vikings. He routed them utterly at Stamford Bridge, on the 24th September; and then, when the weather was mild and serene, and a brilliant sun was shining on the snow-white cliffs of England and on the waters of the Channel, Duke William and his army crossed that open strip of sea, and landed on the undefended shore, at convenient points between Bexhill and Winchelsea, on the feast of St. Michael, the patron of Normandy.

Carefully watching the disembarkation of his troops and their mailed horses, William was the last who stepped on the shore. He stumbled and fell as he did so, and rose with his gauntlets covered with mud, which being deemed a bad omen by some of those about him, he said, "What is the matter? I have thus "taken seisin of this land; and so far as it reaches, by the splendour of God, it is yours and is mine!"

Concentrating his forces on the green slopes at Hastings, he formed an entrenched camp, and set up "two wooden castles," by which are perhaps meant simply palisaded ramparts. Bodies of his mailed cavalry now overran the adjacent country, pillaging and burning the timber-built houses of the people, who sought in vain to hide their goods and cattle in the forests. Some sought refuge in the churches and burial-places, but even there they were massacred without mercy by the Normans. Yet, in addition to the consecrated banner, William wore on his right hand a ring sent him by the Pope, with one of St. Peter's hairs set in it; and thus, as Hume remarks, all the ambition and violence of this invasion were safely covered over by the broad mantle of religion. Harold was at York when tidings of it came. His most gallant leaders had perished at Stamford Bridge. That victory was in some measure his ruin, and for years to come the

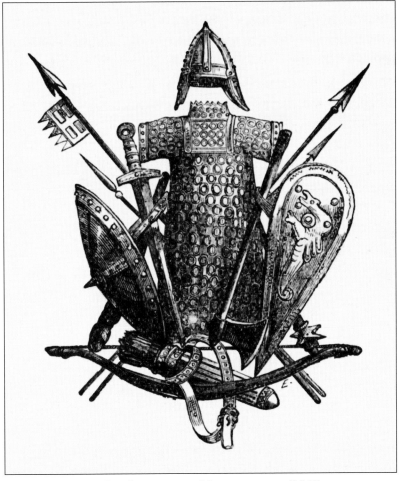

Trophy of Norman and Saxon armour (1066).

ruin of England; and but for the unfortunate landing of Harold Hardrada, Duke William and his Normans might have had another tale to tell of Hastings.

On examining his forces Harold found them sorely cut up and diminished; but though Earl Gurth, his brother, a man of conduct and courage, urged a protraction of the war, Harold, on being reinforced by fresh troops from London and other places, was deaf to his argument, and fired by native courage, elated by victory, and justly incensed by the arrogance of the Normans, he vowed that "he would give battle in person, and convince his subjects that he was worthy of the crown they had set upon his head."' So confident was he of success, that at London he manned 700 ships to prevent the escape of the Normans, and sent a message to the duke offering him a sum of money if he would quit the shores of England without further effusion of blood. This offer William rejected with mocking disdain; and in return sent certain monks requiring him to resign his crown or hold it of him in fealty, to submit their cause to the arbitration of the Pope, or fight him in single combat.

"The God of battles will soon be the great Arbiter of all our differences," was the quiet response of Harold; but he was conscious that dread of the papal excommunication affected his Saxon followers, and perhaps would prevent them making a resolute stand against the invaders. Harold was undoubtedly a man of heroic courage, and had slain many of the Norsemen with his own hand at Stamford Bridge.

He remained six days in London ere he marched against William; and there came with him "Earl Gurth his brother, Earl Leofwin his brother, all his thanes, his franklyns, his housecarles, and the men of London and of Kent, and very many of the men of the southern and eastern shires of England: and the king marched on through the land of the South Saxons, and he came to a hill which men then called Senlac, whereon now is the town of Battle, and there he pitched his camp by the hoar apple tree," which was perhaps some tree held sacred by the Saxons in the days of heathendom.

Accompanied by his brother, Gurth, he rode forward in person to reconnoitre the Norman camp, after having secured his own by palisades. They are said to have quarrelled as to the line of action to be adopted, but to have been silent when they returned as to the subject of dispute.

On the evening of Friday, the 13th October, it was generally known in both armies that a battle would be fought on the morrow. The English were merry; they drank much ale, and were heard singing old Saxon songs: while among the Norman host we are told that the night was passed in prayers and pious processions; and that, notwithstanding the wild, lawless, and warlike spirits which composed it, Odo, Bishop of Bayeux, and Geoffrey, Bishop of Coutances, went through the camp, exhorting to repentance, urging prayer, blessing, and hearing confessions.

Group of Norman soldiers (1066).

On the following morning Duke William rose early, heard mass, and received the holy communion; then gathering around him the leading knights and nobles of his army, he told them that he had come, bent to take that which was his - the crown King Edward had left him - and concluded by reminding them of the ancient prowess of the Normans - how "they had won their land in Gaul with their own swords; how they had given land to the kings of the Franks, and conquered all their enemies everywhere; while the English had never been famed in war, the Danes having conquered them and taken their land whenever they would." This harangue, though probably a fable, is recorded by Henry of Huntingdon and William of Poictiers. Then the whole army marched from Hastings to the hill called Telham, whence they could see the camp of Harold; and then the Norman knights put on their coats of mail, assumed their heavy helmets, and exchanged their light hackneys for their great barbed battle-horses. William, probably in his haste, put on his chain shirt with the back to the front.

"A good sign and a lucky one," said he, laughingly, as he reversed it; "a duke shall this day be turned into a king."

The present aspect of the field is very different now from that which it presented on Harold's birthday, the fatal 14th of October, 1066. No building stood there save a lonely Saxon fane, known as the Church of St. Mary-in-the-Woods, for the use of the peasantry who dwelt in the adjacent forests. The future abbey embraced the centre of Harold's position. His standard waved on Senlac Hill, and on a similar eminence was that of William. Between these a beautiful valley of green meadows and luxuriant woods winds away in a north-easterly direction towards Hastings, where it meets the sea. Then the plain was all desolate and wild.

William rode a Spanish barb; he wore a surcoat above his chain-mail, and a case of holy relics at his neck, and carried in his right hand a truncheon of steel. By his side rode Toustain the Fair, bearing the beautiful banner which Pope Alexander had blessed - a perilous honour, which two barons had declined.

The formation of the Norman army was altogether peculiar. It was drawn up in three long lines. The first, formed of archers and light infantry, was led by Roger de Montgomerie; the second, composed of heavily-mailed men-at-arms, was led by Martel; and the third, led by William in person, was entirely composed of cavalry - knights with their squires, and - yeomen - and its length was so vast that it far outflanked the first two. Splinted armour had not been introduced; the Normans therefore wore tippets and shirts or hauberks of minute iron rings, with, high saddles and steel frontlets for their horses. There was a strong resemblance between the military equipments of the Normans and Saxons at this period; and though the latter wore tunics of iron rings, much of their armour was composed of leather only, and consisted of overlapping flaps, generally stained of different colours, .and shaped like scales or leaves. It was called *corium* by the writers in the succeeding century, and *corietum* in the Norman law. In addition to the ringed byrne, the Saxons had a kind of mail composed of iron bosses sewn on leather, and the short mantle added grace to the figure; while the cross'-gartering, composed of thong, gave a lightness and firmness to their footing. The Saxons wore their hair and beard long and flowing; the Normans had the former shorn and the latter closely shaven.

There was a tribe in Wales then named the Venta, who excelled with the bow, and that weapon is frequently referred to in the poems of Ossian; but save during the Heptarchy, when we read that Offrid, son of the King of Northumbria, was killed by an arrow in a battle fought in 633, near Hatfield, in Yorkshire, little relating to the bow appears in the Saxon annals.

Harold drew up his army in order of battle on a rising mound, with his flanks and front protected by deep trenches, intending to sustain an attack, but avoid, if possible, the heavy-armed cavalry, a force in which he was inferior. In rear of the trenches were ballistae and other engines for casting stones.

In the centre was his royal standard, depicting a warrior in the act of fighting, worked in gold and studded with precious stones, perhaps the handiwork of his queen, Algitha, or of *Swans-hause* ("Edith with the Swan's Throat"), whom Harold loved so well when he was Earl of the East Angles. Besides this, the English had one other great banner, charged with the golden dragon of Wessex.

The Kentish men formed his first line, together with the Londoners, who guarded the standard. All these men were mailed, and armed with javelins, swords, and heavy battle-axes; but the other troops who came from the south and east had no iron defensive armour - few had swords, bows, or axes, and many had pikes, pitchforks, or anything they could get wherewith to arm them. Harold dismounted, with his brothers Leofwin and Gurth; and there on foot, with his battle-axe in his hand, stood the last Saxon king of England, prepared to conquer or die, beside his standard, on the very spot where the high altar of the future minster- rose, and where then there was amid the waste nought but "the hoar apple tree."

Precisely at nine o'clock the whole Norman army began to move forward in three great lines, all marching in unison, and loading the air with the hymn or battle-song of Roland, the peer of Charlemagne, who fell at Roncesvalles. This song was led by Taillefer, or "Cut-iron," the minstrel, who rode in front, tossing up his sword and catching it. With the morning sun shining on the arms and armour of 60,000 men, those lines came down the green slope, their parti-coloured pennons and banners waving, their grey but glittering shirts of mail, and their gaudy surcoats of silk or fine linen, embroidered or painted with the heraldic

Harold at the Battle of Hastings.

cognisances which from that day forward were to be those of the future aristocracy of England.

The Normans came on with spirit and alacrity, and ere long the clouds of arrows and cross-bow bolts' filled the air from both front lines. "God is our help!" was their cry, as they flung themselves against the palisades which fringed the edge of Harold's trench protecting his front, and strove with mailed hands to tear them up and force an entrance for their cavalry.

"Christ's Rood! The Holy Rood!" was the incessant battle-cry of the Saxons, who shot their arrows thick and fast, hurled their javelins, and hewed with their axes, cleaving shields of iron and hauberks of tempered steel asunder. Many fell fast before and behind that formidable palisade, and the Norman writers tell us how dreadful the fight was, "and how the English axe in the hand of King Harold, or any other strong man, cut down the horse and his rider by a single blow."

Harold and his brother fought there among the foremost. He lost an eye by an arrow, and though consequently half blind and in agony, he still continued to fight; while William ordered his archers to press forward, and "instead of shooting with level aim" to discharge their arrows with a curve, so that they might assail the English rear. Horse and foot, knight and pikemen, now poured like a living tempest sheathed in iron on the Saxon trenches.

"Our Lady of help! God be our help!" was the cry; but so terrible was the execution done by the English battle-axes, mauls, and spears, that they were driven down into the ravine between the two hills, where men and horses, killed, wounded) or dying, rolled over each other pell-mell, and many men were even smothered in their armour and their own blood. William had three horses killed under him, and on the third occasion a cry arose that he was slain. On this he remounted and rode along the now shattered line, with his helmet in his hand, that all might see him, exclaiming, "I am here - look at me! I live, and, by God's help, shall conquer!"

Aided by his half-brother, Bishop Odo, he rallied his troops, and once more they returned to the attack with greater fury; the palisades were torn up and an entrance forced for the living mass of men and horses that poured through. The tide of battle began then to verge from the hill .to the heath near the village of Epiton, northward of the present town of Hastings. In dense masses, however, and fighting desperately, the English threw themselves around the standard, and Duke William hewed his way towards it, intent on meeting Harold face to face - a result he never achieved; though Earl Gurth, who fought near his royal

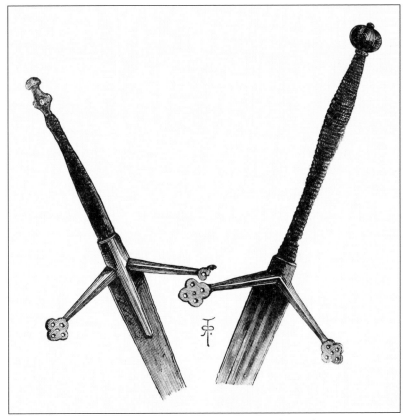

Early Scottish claymores in Warwick Castle.

brother, hurled a spear at the duke, who a few minutes after slew him with his own hand. Earl Leofwin fell next under the sword of Roger de Montgomerie; but still the half-blind Harold stood, axe in hand, beside his standard, with the orb of his shield full of Norman arrows.

Twenty knights now swore to take the standard or die in the attempt, just as Harold fell disabled and faint with loss of blood. Ten fell; among these was Robert Fitz-Ernest, whose skull was cloven by a battle-axe at the moment his hand was on the pole. However, the survivors succeeded in tearing down the English-standard, and planting in its stead the consecrated one which had come from Rome. The golden dragon, "that ancient ensign, which had shone over so many battlefields, was never again borne before a true English king," as it, too, fell into the hands of the Normans. Then four knights, one of whom was Count Eustace of Boulogne, rushed upon Harold as he lay dying. They recognised him by his rich armour and royal insignia, and barbarously killed him with many wounds, sorely mangling his body.

Still the fight was not done, nor was it over till the setting of the sun, for the housecarles and other picked Saxon warriors fought with the courage that is born of vengeance and despair, in deep and miry ground, broken and disordered, against the mighty force of the Norman chivalry. No prisoners were taken, neither did any Saxon take flight till darkness came on, and by that time there lay on the field of Hastings 15,000 Norman dead, and a still greater number of the vanquished, stated at "threescore thousand Englishmen," which is certainly an exaggeration of the truth.

In their riotous joy at having obtained such a victory, when weary of tracking the fugitives by the light of the moon, the Normans exultingly caracoled their horses over the bodies; while William, ordering a place to be cleared of them, pitched a great pavilion, wherein he feasted the principal nobles and knights of his army.

Next day he permitted the bodies of the English to be carried away for burial; and though Hume records that he generously restored the dead body of Harold without ransom to his mother, Gurtha, we now know that though she offered him "Harold's weight in gold, that she might have his body to bury at the Holy Rood of Waltham," William of Poictiers, a trustworthy writer, distinctly records that the Conqueror gave a stem refusal, and ordered it to be buried under a heap of stones on the beach, adding, with a sneer which must have been bitter to every English heart, "He guarded the coast while he was alive, let him thus continue to guard it after death."

Another version is that his mangled body was found on the field by "Edith with the Swan's Throat," who recognised it by a mark on the flesh; and that she had it carefully and tenderly interred under a cairn near the rocks at Hastings, where it lay till the heart of William relented, and it was interred in Harold's own minster at Waltham. There was a favourite fable or story long treasured by the English, to the effect that Harold survived the battle, and lived long years after as an anchorite in a cell near the church of St. John, at Chester - obviously a ridiculous fiction; though Knighton asserts that when the recluse lay dying he owned himself to be Harold, and that the inscription on his tomb was to the same effect.

So ended the great field of Hastings - the last invasion of the island of Great Britain, save the terrible battle of Largs, in 1263, when the Norwegian army was totally destroyed by the Scots - a field which in one day made the proud and imperious Normans lords of all England, from the Channel to the border mountains.

CHAPTER II

THE BATTLE OF THE STANDARD, 1138

THE NEXT great battle fought on English ground is very remarkable from the circumstance that in the component parts of the invading force were represented nearly all of the various races which are now welded together as the British people; and it is of this field that, in Scott's splendid fiction, Cedric the Saxon boasts so justly that the war-cry of his subjugated race was heard as far amid the ranks of the foe as the *cri de guerre* of the proudest Norman baron.

When Henry I, one of the most accomplished princes that ever filled the English throne, died by an unlucky overgorge of lampreys, in 1138, at St. Denis, in Normandy, England had again the prospect of a succession to be disputed in blood. By will he left his kingdom to his daughter Matilda, widow of the Emperor Henry V of Germany; and as the nobles of England and of Normandy had sworn fealty to her, she had every reason to expect the inheritance as queen of both states. But the fierce feudal barons had an aversion to female succession; the feeling was so strong that it prevailed over their oaths and their good faith, and prepared the way for the usurpation of Stephen, Count of Blois, third son of Adela, daughter of the victor of Hastings, who claimed the vacant throne in opposition to Maud, urging that he was the first prince of the blood, and that it was disgraceful for men to submit to a woman's rule. His brother, Henry, Bishop of Winchester, gained for him the leading clergy, and he was joyfully received by the citizens of London, after he had escorted the embalmed body of Henry to the Abbey of Reading, where, on the interment day, he lent his shoulder to bear the leaden coffin.

The first to draw his sword for Maud was her uncle, David I, King of Scotland. Thrice in one year he ravaged with great severity all Northumberland, which he claimed as his own, and on the third occasion he marched as far as Yorkshire. On the approach of Stephen with an army, he deemed it advisable to fall back on Roxburgh, where he took up a strong position, and prepared to give battle; but Stephen, on discovering that some of his nobles had a secret understanding with the enemy, avoided the snare that was laid for him, and, after laying waste the Scottish frontier, retreated south.

In March, 1138, David, re-entered Northumberland, urged, it is supposed, by letters from his niece, the Empress Maud, the justice of whose claim to the throne of England he felt keenly, as she was the only legitimate daughter of King Henry. At the same time, curiously enough, he was uncle to the queen of Stephen.

England was at this time in a very deplorable condition, and the inhabitants of her northern counties had few other resources on which to rely than their own valour and the good policy of Thurstan, the aged Archbishop of York, who, in his decrepit form, displayed all the energy of a youthful warrior. Stephen was so pressed in the South of England, where many of the barons had risen in opposition to his government, that he could raise no army of any consequence to oppose the invading Scots, who mustered 26,000 men; and the only succour he could send to the north was a body of lances under Bernard de Baliol, a Yorkshire baron, whose 'descendants were afterwards to bear a prominent; and ignoble part in Scottish history. But Thurstan had already assembled the northern barons, exhorting them "to fight for their families and I their God; he assured them of victory, and promised heaven to those who might fall in so sacred a cause." Aged, and unable to appear in public on account of many infirmities, this noble old prelate deputed an ecclesiastic named Ralph Nowel, whom, in the exercise of his usurped authority over the Scottish Church, he had named Bishop of Orkney, to act as his representative. The archbishop issued an order for all the ecclesiastics in every parish of his diocese to appear in procession, with their crosses, banners, and relics, and enjoined all men capable of bearing arms to repair to the general rendezvous of the northern barons at Thirsk, in defence of Christ's Church against the barbarians. Three days were spent in fasting and devotion; on the fourth Thurstan made them swear never to desert each other in the coming strife. He promised victory to all who were penitent. At York he heard the confessions of the barons, and delivered into their hands his crozier and his metropolitan banner, which was dedicated to St. Peter. The chiefs who came were William, Earl of Albemarle, Robert de Ferrars, William Percy, Roger de Mowbray, Ilbert de Lacy, and Walter l'Espec, an aged Norman warrior of great experience.

Meanwhile the Scots were coming on with sword and with flame. David detached his nephew, William, at the head of a body of Galloway men, into the West of England, where, on the 4th of June, he defeated a considerable force near Clitheroe, and carried off much spoil. The king by this time had laid siege to the strong castle of Norham, which Ralph Flambard, Bishop of Durham, had erected nineteen years before to repress the inroads of the Scottish borderers; it was surrendered, and dismantled by David, who marched south through Northumberland and Durham without opposition, till he came to Alverton, now called Northallerton, in the North Riding of Yorkshire, on the 22nd of August.

The English army was drawn up in array of battle on Cutton Moor, close by this place. It was then a wide waste of purple heather, dark green gorse, and stunted bushes. There they had erected a remarkable standard, consisting of the mast of a ship securely lashed to a four-wheeled car or wain. On the summit of this mast was placed a large crucifix, having in its centre a silver box containing the consecrated host, and below it waved the banners of three patron saints - Peter of York, Wilfred of Ripon, and John of Beverley. Hence the name of the conflict, the "Battle of the Standard."

Walter L'Espec and the Earl of Albemarle.

At its base, sheathed in armour, with his helmet open, old Walter l'Espec harangued his followers; and, at the conclusion of his speech, gave his ungauntleted hand to William, Earl of Albemarle exclaiming, "I pledge thee my troth to conquer or to die!"

These words kindled a great enthusiasm among the fiery spirits around him, and the oath of fealty So each other was then repeated by all. The representative of the energetic old Thurstan delivered a - speech for the encouragement of the army. It opened thus, according to Matthew of Paris: - "Illustrious chiefs of England, by blood and race Normans, before whom France trembles - to whom fair England has submitted - under whom Apulia has been restored to her station - and whose names are famous at Antioch and Jerusalem; here are the Scots, who fear you, undertaking to drive you from your estates!"

The three lines of the Scots were now in sight; and on a signal being given, the whole English knelt while the representative of Thurstan read from the carriage the prayer of absolution. With' a universal shout, they answered "Amen," and then every man repaired to his place. From the Conquest to the close of the twelfth century but little change had taken place in the armour and weapons of the English; but five distinct varieties of body-armour were worn by them about the time of the Standard - a scaly suit of steel, with a *chapelle de fer*, or iron cap; a hauberk of iron rings; a suit of mascled or quilted armour; another of rings set edgewise; and a fifth of tegulated mail, composed of small square plates of steel lapping over each other like tiles, with a long flowing tunic of cloth below. Gonfanons fluttered from the spear-heads; and knights wore nasal helmets and kite-shaped shields of iron, but their spears were simply pointed goads.

Though the red lion had been one national emblem of the Scots for more than a hundred years, and traditionally the thistle for a much longer period, on this day the standard borne by them was simply a long lance with a tuft of blooming mountain-heather attached to it; and the armour and equipment of the Lowlanders were pretty much like those of the English. The vanguard consisted of the men of Lothian and Teviotdale, the moss-troopers of Liddesdale and Cumberland, and the fierce and wild men of Galloway under their principal chiefs, Ulric and Donald, led by Prince Henry, who was reinforced by a body-guard of men-at-arms under Eustace Fitzjohn, a Norman baron of Northumberland, whom Stephen had offended by depriving him of the castle of Bamborough.

The second line was composed of the Highland and Island clans, armed with their round targets, two-handed claymores, and *tuaghs* or pole-axes. The third, or reserve line, under the king, consisted of a strong body of Saxon and Norman knights and men-at-arms, with the men of Moray and from other parts covering the rear. Such was the singularly mixed force led by the Scottish king; for in his ranks were many men of England who favoured the cause of his niece the empress, or were disgusted with Stephen's rule at home.

Favoured by a dense fog and the smoke of burning villages, which concealed his advance for a time, he was not without hope of taking the English by surprise; but they were fully prepared, and everyman stood to his arms. Ere the battle began, the Norman barons, inspired by a humanity somewhat new to them, sent to the Scottish army Robert Bruce, Earl of Annandale, and Bernard de Baliol, nobles who held vast estates in both countries, to offer as conditions of peace "to procure from Stephen a full grant of the earldom of Northumberland in favour of Prince Henry."

The speech of Bruce, which was long, and contains many curious facts, is reported at length by Aired, a contemporary and confidant of David, hence it may be assumed to be substantially accurate; but David rejected all proposals.

Then exclaimed William MacDonoquhy, his nephew, "Bruce, thou art a false traitor! "Whereupon Bruce and Baliol departed, renouncing their allegiance to the Scottish crown, and the advance was resumed. The king, resolving now to place some Norman knights and Saxon arch era in the van, gave terrible offence to the bare-kneed Celts who were in his army, and it threatened the most disastrous consequences.

"Whence comes this mighty confidence in those Normans?" asked Malise, Earl of Stratheam, scornfully. "I wear no armour; but there is not one among them who will advance beyond me this day."

"Rude earl," replied Allan de Piercy, a Norman knight, "you boast of what you dare not do."

David had to interfere, and place the Celtic clans of Galloway in the van, and reserve to himself the command of the Scots properly so called.

The English were drawn up in a dense mass around the sacred standard. Their men-at-arms dismounted, and sending their horses to the rear, mingled with the archers, and met the shock of battle on foot. It was begun by the fierce "wild men," as they were named, of Galloway, who flung themselves sword in hand on the serried English spears with shouts of "*Albanaich! Albanaich!*" which means, "We are the men of Albyn!" The spearmen gave way; but a heavy shower of arrows threw the Celts into disorder, and as they fell back the English taunted them by shouting, "*Erygh! Erygh !*" ("Ye are but Irish! ye are but Irish!")

Prince Henry now rushed on at the head of his mailed cavalry, charging with lances levelled, and broke through the English ranks, says Aired, "as if they had been spiders' webs," and actually dispersed those who guarded the horses in the rear. Ulric and Donald had fallen, yet the Galloway men rallied without them, and renewed the attack; the other lines were closing up, and for two hours the battle was but one wild mêlée of men and horses wedged and struggling together. Thus far one account. Another says that it was in vain that the Scots, "after giving three shouts in the manner of their nation," sought with their swords to break through the forest of spears. "Their courage only exposed them to the deadly aim of the archers; and at the end of two hours, disheartened by their loss, they wavered, broke, and fled."

The story goes that when the Galloway men rallied, and with terrible yells were about to renew the attack, an English soldier, with singular tact and presence of mind, suddenly elevated a human head upon his spear, and shouted, "Behold the head of the King of the Scots!"

This spread speedy consternation, and the men of Galloway fled, falling back upon the second line, while the third abandoned the field without striking a blow. On foot, David strove to rally them, but in vain: then his knights and men-at-arms, perceiving that the day was lost, constrained him to quit the field. Placing himself at their head, he covered the retreat and prevented the pursuit of his ill-matched army as far as Carlisle, when, enraged by their defeat and the loss of some thousands of their number, fired with mutual animosities and petty national jealousies, they assaulted each other, and fought promiscuously among themselves.

It was on the 25th August that David entered Carlisle, and there for some days he was in great uncertainty as to the fate of his gallant son, Prince Henry, whose impetuosity had carried him through the ranks of the English. "On his return from the chase of fugitives in the rear, finding the battle lost, he commanded his men to throw away their banners, and so mingling with the pursuers, he passed them undiscovered, and after many hazards succeeded in reaching Carlisle on the third day after the king his father."

In their retreat the Galloway men carried off many Englishwomen, who were only restored through the intervention of Alberic, Bishop of Ostia, the papal legate, a circumstance which affords some proof of the barbarity of the times, and the ferocity of the troops who carried on the war. Yet David who led them was founder of twelve of the most magnificent abbeys in Scotland. At Carlisle he exacted a solemn oath from all that they should never again desert him in war; and after storming and razing to the ground Walter l'Espec's castle of Werk, he returned to Scotland more like a conqueror than one whose army had been so totally routed, as the victors of Northallerton were not in a condition to follow up the- advantage they had gained; and, ultimately, through the mediation of the legate and the Queen of England, peace was concluded on the 9th April, 1139.

The old monastic writers of England dwelt with great satisfaction on the singular battle of the Standard, which they considered to have been won, less by-the valour and hardihood of those who fought under old Walter l'Espec of Werk, than the influence of the holy relics and the banners of St. Peter of York, St. Wilfred of Ripon, and St. John of Beverley. The place where they stood is still called the Standard Hill at Northallerton.

DAMME - BOUVINES - DOVER, 1214 - 1217

DAMME

I T IS somewhat remarkable that it is in the time of King John, whom an English historian has justly characterised as "a mean coward, a shameless liar, the most profligate of a profligate age, and the most faithless of a faithless race," that we find those two great historical facts, the assertion of English supremacy over the sea, and the first great naval engagement between the French and English - a brilliant spot in the gloomy history of his time, and from which may be traced that series of bright naval exploits which have been our boast for ages, and, let us hope, may long continue to be so, after the "wooden walls "have passed away, or given place to those of iron.

The leading causes of the first great naval battle were as follows: - John having divorced Joanna, married Isabella of Angoulgme. This, with the murder of Arthur, roused his enemies against him, and they speedily stripped him of Normandy, and all that the Plantagenet kings once held in France. His quarrel with the Pope drew upon England the spiritual terrors of an interdict, and for six years there was no religious service in the land; the churches were closed, the unused bells hung rusting in their spires; the statues of the saints were draped in black, and the dead were interred without prayer or ceremony, while the living were under a curse. This state of matters caused Philip Augustus of France, a wily and ambitious sovereign, to conceive the idea of invading England, and annexing it as a fief to his crown. That which William of Normandy had done before, might it not be done again? The opportunity was most favourable, and accordingly he made such great preparations for the complete conquest of England, at the call of the Pope too, that John, hitherto unmoved, yielded; and sensible that of the 60,000 soldiers whom he called his, not one was to be trusted, he took a new oath of fealty to the pontiff, and agreed to pay into his coffers 1,000 marks yearly rent for his kingdom of England and lordship of Ireland,

This was in 1213, and now he took vigorous measures for rallying round him a large body of his subjects, and by the middle of April he had a great fleet as well as a large army assembled at Dover. The French monarch had determined to chastise Ferrand, Count of Flanders, for refusing to join with him in this expedition against England, and forming a secret treaty with John, who sent him armed aid. For this purpose he marched into the Low Countries, while his fleet sailed from the Seine to the Damme, an old town five miles from Bruges, on a canal of the same name, which extends from the latter city to Moerkerke.

The fleet is said to have numbered 1,700 sail; and to anticipate and destroy all attempt at invasion, that of the English, consisting of only 500 sail, put to sea under Henry II's son by the fair Rosamond Clifford, William with the Long Sword, Earl of Salisbury; John's brother, the Duke of Holland; and the Count de Boulogne. The vessels of those days were but small. Their masts were usually made in one piece; the sails were large and square; the tops were large round turrets, where archers and crossbow-men lurked; the sides were always furnished with iron grapnels; the poops and prows were high; and the knights on board were wont to hang their shields around the gunwale before assuming them for battle. Long sweeps at times aided the sails, and around the masts were usually racked the axes and pikes of the crew.

According to De Mezeray, when Salisbury with his fleet

appeared off the Damme, he found a great many of Philip's vessels at anchor in the roadstead, with most of their crews ashore. Others were moored inside the harbour and along the coast. Be all that as it may, he ordered an immediate attack on those in the roads; and in a very short time the English captured 300 sail - 100 more of a small size were lying high and dry upon the beach. These were pillaged of all they contained and all that could be carried off, and were then set on flames. In their boats the English seamen next assailed the vessels lying within the harbour; "and those Frenchmen," says old Holinshed, "that were gone into the country, perceiving that their enemies were come by the running away of the mariners, returned with all speed to their ships to aid their fellows, and so made valiant resistance for a time, till the Englishmen, getting on land and ranging themselves on either side of the haven, beat the Frenchmen on

Advance of the English fleet upon Damme.

both sides; and the ships being grappled together in front, they fought on the decks as it had been in a pitched field, till that finally the Frenchmen were not able to sustain the force of the Englishmen, but were constrained, after long fighting and great slaughter, to yield themselves prisoners."

There was a considerable number of ships in a dock higher up the harbour, and for the purpose of attacking these the English, now flushed with triumph, made an assault upon the town of Bruges, but were repulsed after a sharp engagement, and had to retreat to their ships with the loss of 2,000 men. Such was the effect of this engagement, in which so many vessels were taken, sunk, or burnt, and the city of the Damme given to the flames, that Philip, in a gust of fury, burned the remainder of his fleet and quitted Flanders.

Such was the result of the first engagement between the fleets of France and England; and thus, under Lord Salisbury, was inaugurated a long series of naval glories. It is in Chaucer that we find the first description of an English sailor during the early part of the fourteenth century, and still in some points it is characteristic of the profession. He tells us how his shipman rode upon a hackney as best he could; he wore a gown of raiding, or coarse cloth, to his knee -

"A dagger hanging by a lace had he
About his neck, under his arm adown.
The hot summer had made his face all brown;
And certainly he was a good fellow -
Full mony a draught of wine he hadde draw.

He knew well all the havens as they were
From Gothland to the Cape de Finisterre,
And every creek in Britain and in Spain;
His barge ycleped was the *Magdalen*,"

BOUVINES

By the repulse at the Damme the schemes of Philip Augustus against England were baffled for a time, and this, together with the fact of many men of Poitou and Anjou seeking an asylum in England, so encouraged John, that in the first flush of success he sailed for Poitou, in the hope of creating a diversion in favour of the Count of Flanders; but his hope of doing anything brilliant was blasted by the defeat of the latter, with the English forces under the Earl of Salisbury sent to his aid, and those of the Emperor Olho, at Bouvines, a little village between Lille and Tournay, where, on the 27th July, 1214, was fought one of the most decisive battles of the age.

There came the Emperor Otho, the Earl of Flanders, the Dukes of Lorraine and Brabant, and Longsword, Earl of Salisbury, at the head of 120,000 men. The King of France had not nearly so many; Galon de Montigny was his standard-bearer. It was on this occasion that the French first began to use the cross-bow, invented in the days of Louis le Gros; but it lay with the heavy cavalry, who were armed cap-a-pie, to decide the fate of the day. As for the infantry, they wore here what defensive armour they pleased; their weapons being the sword, the bow, the mace, and the sling of classical antiquity.

Guerin, Bishop of Senlis, formerly a knight of St. John of Jerusalem, drew up the French army in order of battle; and the famous Bishop of Beauvais, who was so long the prisoner of Richard of England, rode near him armed with a ponderous mace, as he alleged that it was "against the canons to spill human blood;" but there is no record in history of the mode or manner in which either the emperor or king ranged their troops. Before they closed in battle, the latter ordered that the 68th Psalm, *Exsurgat Dens, et dissipentur inimici ejus* ("Let God arise, let his enemies be scattered"), should be sung along the whole line, in lieu of the song of Roland; as if Otho was in arms against the Almighty.

Like the English standard at Northallerton, that of Otho was fixed in a four-wheeled chariot; it was a green dragon, surmounted by an imperial eagle of wood, richly gilded. On the other side, the royal standard of France was a gilded staff, with white silk colours, powdered with silver lilies. Besides this, they had the oriflamme, which was, as its name imports, a flame-coloured banner, on a cross staff uncharged, divided at its lower edge into three parts, each furnished with a green tassel. It was always lodged in the Abbey of St. Denis, and never unfurled save when a king of France took the field; and whenever he was in danger, one or other of the standards was lowered.

Many thousand knights' pennons, square and swallow-tailed, were rustling in the wind as these great armies closed in the mortal shock; the Germans shouting "Kyrie eleison," and the French "Montjoye St. Denis! "

Fortune-tellers had predicted, says De Mezeray, to the old Countess of Flanders, "that the king should be overthrown, and horses tread him down; but that her nephew Ferrand should enter Paris in triumph." The first part of this prediction became true, for Philip was unhorsed in the first charge, and received blows on all sides from swords, maces, and lances, but was saved unscathed by his armour, though a German *reiter* strove to pierce his neck with a javelin. Ferrand was afterwards taken, and literally entered Paris, but loaded with chains, in an open chariot drawn by four grey horses. Otho was routed, with the loss of 30,000 men; his imperial standard was taken, and the chariot that bore it was hewed to pieces with battle-axes; and he died soon after of grief. He had five great nobles taken prisoners, one of whom was the hero of the Damme, Longsword, Earl of Salisbury (whom the Bishop of Beauvais beat down with his mace), and twenty knight bannerets, according to the Chronicle of Melrose, Matthew Paris, and others; but only one knight fell, William Long-champ, who was killed by a thrust through the visor of his helmet. The mace was then the usual weapon of churchmen when they went to battle; but knights carried it at the right side of the saddlebow, and seldom used it till their sword or lance was broken.

The person who lost most by this battle was King John, and those who ultimately gained most were the English people. The tidings of Bouvines, where his friends, troops, and allies had been so completely routed that no prince dared ever after to withstand Philip Augustus, sent him home inspired with double fury and ferocity; and once more foreign mercenaries were let loose on England, until there came that ever-memorable 15th of June, 1215, when, at Runnymede, a grassy meadow on the banks of the Thames, between Windsor and Staines, the Great Charter of England's liberty was wrested by the justly incensed barons from the most pitiful tyrant that ever sat upon her throne.

DOVER

John's vengeance led to what we are about to narrate, the battle of Dover, another great fight which took place in sight of the shores of England, and which tended still further to assert and to maintain her supremacy on the sea.

No sooner had the barons dispersed their forces and retired to their castles, than John, at the head of a body of Gascon and Poitevin mercenaries, assailed them in succession with a fury and vindictiveness that showed how lightly he valued an oath, and soon the sky was red at night and darkened by day with the blaze of burning towns and cornfields, while the people fled to the hills and forests in despair; and, unless he exaggerates, Matthew of Paris records that this was the state of matters from Dover to Berwick, over all the land. In this extremity, the

English barons took the desperate course of offering the crown to Louis of France, who had married John's niece; and then the horrors of a second Conquest seemed to hang over the divided people, for this Louis was the eldest son of Philip Augustus, and many of the great lords, inspired by a national spirit, were averse to the measure.

With real avidity, but with pretended reluctance, the offer of the English crown was accepted; a French army mustered at Calais, and Louis, with a numerous and well-appointed armament, consisting of 680 ships, set sail for England. Notwithstanding that the barons of the Cinque Ports, who remained faithful to John, attacked and cut off some of his ships on the high seas, he landed safely at Sandwich, on the 30th May, 1216. John was marching to meet him; but on the shores of the Wash the rising tide suddenly swept away all his baggage, jewels, and treasures. Agitation fevered him, and he died, unregretted by his friends, some say of poison, but according to others of a surfeit of peaches and ale. Louis with his adherents held London and the southern counties; but the barons, whose feelings had changed since John's death, rallied round young Henry of Winchester, whom, as the royal crown had perished in the Wash, they crowned with a fillet of gold at Gloucester, and all true Englishmen wore a similar fillet of white cloth in honour of the event. But Louis was determined not to quit the island without a struggle, though forced to abandon all hope after the somewhat petty but otherwise important battle known as the "Fair of Lincoln," on the 19th May, 1217. The little King Henry was only ten years old, and the Earl of Pembroke was appointed Regent.

While Louis, who had lost everything north of London, was cooped up there, a powerful fleet and army were prepared in France for his succour. At Calais, the troops destined for this enterprise, embarked on board of eighty large ships, besides galleys, and other armed and store vessels, the whole under the command of Eustace le Moine (the Monk), a famous sea-rover of those days, who had quitted his cloister for the more congenial scenes of outrage and battle by sea and land.

This dreaded adventurer was born at Cors, in the Boulonnois, and was at one time in the service of King John, during 1205. About the time the Magna Charta was signed, he had collected many vessels, with which he harassed the English in the Channel; but now the time of his punishment was come.

On the 24th of August the French armament put to sea, intending to sail up the Thames, to make spoil of London, and there land their troops, which were under the command of Robert de Courtenay; but "the silver streak" was not to be crossed so easily as in the days of the fated Harold.

Hubert de Burgh - who had been Seneschal of Poitou; whose fourth wife was Margaret, a princess of Scotland; and who was now the Royal Justiciary and Governor of the Castle of Dover, which Louis was besieging - was fully impressed with the necessity of preventing the landing of this formidable force on English ground, and, more than all, their occupation of the capital, and took immediate measures for that purpose.

Addressing Peter de Rupilius, then Bishop of Winchester, the marshal, and other great personages whom he had called round him, he said, emphatically, "If these people land, England is lost. Let us meet them boldly, therefore, for God is with us, and they are excommunicated."

"We are neither sea-soldiers nor pirates," replied his audience, who did not share his ardour, or feared the monk Eustace, "neither are we fishermen. Go thou and die!"

Undiscouraged by this, De Burgh sent for his chaplain, and having hastily taken the sacrament, he put on his armour, and mustering the soldiers of the garrison of Dover, with an emphatic oath, he enjoined them to defend their post to the last, adding, "Ye shall suffer me to be hanged before ye surrender this castle, for it is the key of England."

Affected even to tears by his exhortation, and still more by the fate that seemed to await him, they pledged themselves to obey his commands. There is one other account of this episode, which though a little different is not the less interesting. It is said that when the French fleet was seen by the people of the Cinque Ports, like white birds at the far horizon, knowing it to be commanded by the dreaded Eustace, they said, "If this tyrant land, he will lay all waste, for the country is unprotected, and the king is far away. Let us, therefore, put our souls into our hands, and meet him while he is at sea, and help will come to us from on High."

"Is there any man among you who is this day ready to die for England?" asked another; and a third said, "Here am I." "Then," said the first who spoke, "take with thee an axe, and when thou seest us engaging the tyrant's ship, climb up the mast and cut down his banner, so that the other vessels may be dispersed for want of a leader."

Sixteen ships belonging to the Cinque Ports, and about twenty smaller vessels, formed the English squadron. With the bravest of his knights, Sir Philip d'Albany (Governor of Jersey), Sir Henry de Tuberville, Sir Richard Suuard, Richard, a natural son of King John, and others, De Burgh, committing the defence of Dover to his second in command, led them on board, and they put to sea; and from the white cliffs that overlooked it they were watched by thousands of anxious eyes.

The enemy's fleet of eighty sail - a terrible disparity in strength and number - was already some miles off Calais when the English ships bore towards them, with all their gay banners flying; their square lug-sails, some brown, some gaudily dyed and painted; their high poops and forecastles having doors pointed like those of chapels, and studded with nails like those of prisons; their hulls built in that quaint form still adhered to by the Dutch; and each bristling from stem to stern with arms and armour. "But all the accounts of this engagement," says Sir Harris Nicholas, "are defective in nautical details, while the few that do occur are very obscurely expressed."

De Burgh's oath.

It appears that the wind was southerly, blowing fresh, and the French were going large, i.e., with the breeze abaft the beam, steering to round the North Foreland, and not expecting much if any opposition. So the English squadron, instead of directly approaching them, kept their wind as if bound for Calais harbour; then Eustace, the commander, exclaimed, "I know what these wretches think - they will invade Calais like thieves; but that is useless, as it is well defended."

So each bore on, but as soon as the little fleet of old England - it was "old England "then as now - got the weather-gage of the French, they suddenly bore down in the most gallant manner upon their rear; and the moment they came athwart the sterns of the French ships, they threw their grapnels into them, and thus preventing the enemy from escaping, held them fast - an early instance of that wild love of close fighting for which English sailors have ever been distinguished.

The battle began by the crossbow-men and archers, under Sir Philip d'Albany, pouring volleys of bolts and arrows into the enemy's ships fore and aft with deadly effect; and, to increase their dismay, as cannon were still unknown, the English threw sacksful of unslaked lime, reduced to fine powder, onboard their antagonists, which being blown by the wind into their eyes, completely blinded them. With pike, dagger, and axe, the English now poured on board in a torrent, and cutting away the rigging and halyards, the sails with all their top-hamper fell over the French, to use the expression of an old historian, "like a net upon ensnared small birds," and thus trammelled they could make but a feeble resistance. After an immense slaughter they were completely defeated; for though the French were unquestionably brave, they were less accustomed to naval tactics and to fighting upon the water than their assailants, beneath whose lances, axes, and swords they fell rapidly.

Disdaining to be taken alive, or more probably dreading

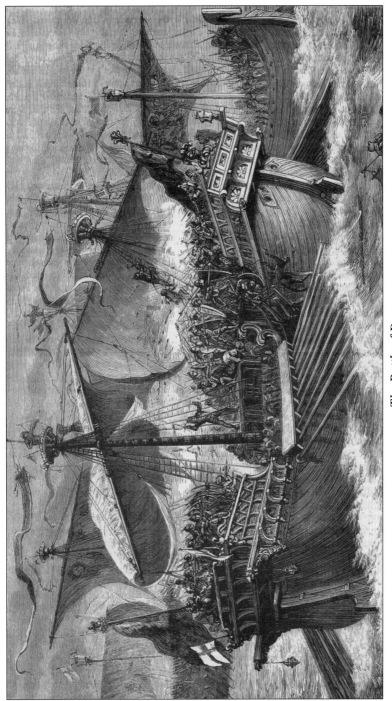

The Battle of Dover.

to fall into the hands of the English, whose custom it was to treat prisoners with great severity, that they might be induced to pay exorbitant sums as ransom, many noble French knights leaped into the sea in their heavy armour, and were never seen again. Matthew Paris records that Eustace the Monk was seized by Richard, the son of King John, who by one slash of his sword hewed off his head. Of his whole fleet only fifteen vessels escaped; and with the remaining sixty-five in tow, or under prize crews, De Burgh and his Englishmen returned to Dover; and we are told that, "while victoriously ploughing the waves," they devoutly returned thanks to God for their success, an example of simple religious gratitude after battle which has been followed by our tars often in more modern times.

Prior to his death, Eustace the Monk is said to have hidden himself in some secret cabin, and when found offered a large sum of money as ransom for his life, promising at the same time to serve Henry of Winchester faithfully for the future; on which Richard exclaimed, as he slew him, "Base traitor, never again shall you seduce any one by your false promises."

His head was afterwards carried through England on a pole. There was no cannon-smoke to obscure the air then, and there were no telescopes to peer through; but the battle was witnessed, under a bright August sun, with exultation by the people and garrison of Dover, and the victors were welcomed by the bishops and clergy in full sacerdotal vestments, bearing banners and crosses in procession, chanting praises to God for the rescue of England. Gold, silver, silken garments, rich armour, and weapons, the spoil of the foe, having been collected, and the prisoners disposed of, Sir Philip d'Albany was dispatched to the boy king and the Regent Pembroke, with tidings of "this glorious naval victory, which secured the independence of England."

Among the prisoners taken were Robert de Courtenay,

Ralph de Tornellis, William de Barrés, 125 knights, and more than 6,000 men-at-arms; while De Burgh's loss, being nowhere mentioned, cannot have been very great. Sir Philip d'Albany died when performing a second pilgrimage to the Holy Land, in 1237.

One of the most immediate and important results of this battle was that Louis relinquished his claim to the throne of England, and quitted its shores, but not without reluctance, and certain stipulations for the safety of his friends; thus ending a civil war which seemed to be founded on the most incurable hatred and jealousy, and which had threatened England with the most fatal consequences: and when Pembroke died, in the third year of his regency, the government of the country was divided between the Bishop of Winchester and the victor in the battle off Dover, who was made Lord High Admiral of England.

Ultimately he was very ill requited for all his services. On false charges, the year 1224 saw him a prisoner in the Tower of London, from whence he was removed to a dungeon in the castle of Devizes; and after many vicissitudes, he died at Banstead, in Surrey, on the 12th May, 1243.

CHAPTER IV

LEWES, 1264 - EVESHAM, 1265 - IN THE CHANNEL, 1293

LEWES

FRANCE WAS now in no way disposed to meddle with England; and during the long reign of Henry the sword was never drawn with Scotland, though there were several disputes as to which kingdom should possess Cumberland, Northumberland, and Westmoreland.

The King's fondness for the Poictevins and the Provençals, who flocked after his consort, Eleanor, roused, however, the jealousy of the nation, and ere long the barons revolted, under Simon de Montfort, Earl of Leicester, who had married the king's sister, Eleanor; and this, together with the departure of his younger brother, Richard, to win laurels in the fourth Crusade, and win the crown of the Romans, shook the throne of England, and raised the secret hopes of those who aspired to its overthrow. In 1258, in token of mischief to come, the barons came to council at Westminster sheathed in full armour; and when they assembled at Oxford, in what was called the "Mad Parliament," they appointed a committee of twenty-four restless spirits to reform the state, and these passed certain-enactments which are matters of general history, and were called the "Provisions of Oxford." But the wished-for reforms were delayed by disunion and jealousies among themselves; and the King of France, on being chosen umpire, gave, perhaps naturally, the decision in favour of Henry III. On this the flames of civil war broke forth.

Simon of Leicester held London; and when the great bell of old St. Paul's rang out the alarm, the citizens from Fenchurch, Chepe, and Strand, flocked round his standard to pillage the foreign merchants, whom they deemed fair objects of spoil, and to murder the unhappy Jews - then viewed as all men's prey, and as an accursed race. In the same year a famine increased the troubles of the land.

The year 1264 saw the rival factions nearly equal in number of adherents and in military resources. The northern counties, conspicuous ever in history for reasoning and unreasoning' loyalty, together with those along the Welsh border, declared for the king; while the midland shires, the Cinque Ports, and London, "being the fattest and most attractive baits for the cupidity of foreigners," declared for Leicester. And among those who were- reckoned foreigners were Robert Bruce the elder, Earl of Annandale; John Comyn, Lord of Badenoch; and John Baliol, all Scoto-Normans, who brought their vassals from beyond the borders, as volunteers to Henry's standard.

On the Leicester side were DeWarrene, Gloucester, the De l'Espensers, William Marmion, Robert de Roos, Richard Grey, John Fitz-John, Nicholas Seagrave, and many other nobles of high lineage and large estate; and the politic earl endeavoured to impart a sacred character to his cause, for after recounting to them .-the many alleged perjuries of the king, he assured them that God was on their side, and caused them all to wear white crosses on their surcoats, as if they had been warring in a crusade against heathens, and not Christian Englishmen like themselves. And when the parties drew near each other in order of battle, at Lewes, in Sussex, on the 14th of May, John Arundel, Bishop of Chichester, and formerly a prebend of St. Paul's, went through the insurgent ranks, giving a general absolution to all, and promising heaven to all who might fall.

By this time flat-ringed armour had nearly disappeared, and that composed of rings set edgeways was almost generally worn, with much quilted and padded armour, made of silk, cloth, buckram, and leather; and these materials, from the peculiar manner in which they were ornamented, obtained the name of *pourpoint* and *counterpoint*. The surcoats were usually elaborately emblazoned with the family arms and honours of the wearer. Small plates of steel were beginning to be worn at the shoulders, elbows, and knees, called, according to their position, *epaulières* (hence epaulettes), *coutes*, and *genouillères*, and to these were added in turn splint after splint, till the complete mail of future years was reached. The helmets were barrel-formed, and rested on the shoulders, cumbrous, and liable to be wheeled round by a lance thrust. Iron skullcaps were worn by esquires, archers, and men-at-arms. A knight's shield was straight at the top; and now, in addition to the weapons of the last century, he added a *martel-de-fer*, in fact, a mere pointed hammer, for the purpose of breaking the links of chain-mail and plates, to leave openings for the point of lance or sword; and now, for the first time, the roweled spur had replaced the barbarous goad.

It was on the present race-ground, the down now traditionally known as "Mount Harry," the encounter we are about to narrate took place, near where the ancient town of Lewes, with its walls, and the loftily-situated castle built by William de Warrene, son-in-law of the Conqueror, still stately in ruin, look down on the grassy vales of Sussex and the Ouse winding to the sea.

The royal army was divided into three bodies. Prince Edward had the right; the King of the Romans the left; Henry III led the main body, where his standard, a dragon, was displayed.

The army of the barons was formed in five divisions. The first was led by Henry de Montfort and the Earls of Hereford and Essex; the second by the Earl of Gloucester, with Fitz-John and William de Montcausis; the third was led by the Earl of Leicester; the fourth, consisting wholly of Londoners, was on the extreme left, under Nicholas Seagrave, mustering 15,000 men, according to Matthew of Westminster.

The battle was begun by the young and fiery Prince Edward,

who, at the head of a chosen body of knights and men-at-arrns, with lances in the rest, made a terrible charge on the Londoners. Burning to avenge the insults they had heaped upon his mother, whom they had threatened to drown as a witch, he attacked them with such impetuous fury that they were broken in an instant, driven in disorder from the field, trampled under hoof, and slaughtered in heaps; and for four miles he pursued them without giving quarter to a single man. But this victory cost him dear, as he left the royal infantry totally unprotected; so they in turn were borne down under a combined attack from the columns of Leicester and Gloucester. For a time all were mingled together, fighting "with a fury mixed with despair;" and ultimately the king's forces began to retire towards the foot of that high green hill on which the grey old castle of Lewes stands, many of them hoping there to find shelter and make terms. But - alas for them! - town and castle were alike in the hands of the barons, and finding themselves surrounded on all sides, they surrendered at discretion. So there were taken Henry, King of England; his brother, the King of the Romans; Humphry de Bohun, Earl of Hereford; William Bardolf, Robert de Tattershall, Henry de Piercy, and the three Scottish auxiliaries, Bruce, Baliol, and Comyn.

Young Edward returned from his vengeful pursuit to find the day thus lost, more than 5,000 English corpses covering the ground, and among those of his father's people were De Wilton, the Justiciary, and Fulk Fitz-Warin; and of the barons, 'three noble knights, one of whom was William Blund, their standard-bearer.

For that night the king and his kinsmen were lodged in the Priory of Lewes, some remains of which are still discernible near the town.

In the meantime the queen, Eleanor, who had fled to the Continent, gathered a numerous force with the aid of different princes, who regarded the cause of Henry as their own; and she was now waiting at the Damme, in Flanders, ready to cross the Channel: but Leicester ("Sir Simon the Righteous," as the English called him), with great promptitude, ordered a muster of the barons' troops on Barham Downs to await her landing. He also went on board a fleet to meet her on the sea. This display of resolution, together with the defeat at Lewes, so intimidated the leaders of the queen that they disbanded their land forces, and their fleet never ventured from port.

EVESHAM

Leicester was frequently harassed by solicitations for the release of the two princes, Edward and Henry. At last he pretended to acquiesce, and convoked a Parliament to sanction the measure; though the secret motive was to consolidate his own power, the power which he had won by years of labour, danger, and intrigue. He had hitherto enjoyed the co-operation of the Earls of Derby and Gloucester; but if he was ambitious and casting eyes towards the throne, they were too proud to bow to a fellow-subject Quarrels ensued, and the arrest of the former warning Gloucester of danger, he unfurled the royal standard in the midst of his tenantry; and Leicester immediately marched towards Hereford, carrying with him his prisoners guarded by a numerous body of knights. One day after dinner Prince Edward obtained permission "to breathe two or three horses" in the fields outside the town, attended by certain gentlemen who guarded him continually. After riding to and fro a little space, he suddenly dashed the spurs into the fleetest of the animals which he mounted, and which had been sent to him by the Earl of Gloucester, and ere his guards could recover from their surprise he had fairly escaped.

Prince Edward, with Gloucester, now concerted the plan of

a new campaign; while every day malcontents with Leicester's government came flocking to their standard. The latter's forces were divided, a part remaining with himself at Hereford, while the rest were with his son, Simon de Montfort, in Sussex; so the first object of Edward was to prevent their effecting a junction, by confining the earl to the right bank of the Severn. For this purpose he destroyed all the bridges and sunk all the boats on the river, which was then broader and deeper than it is now: after that he marched against Simon, whose forces he surprised near Kenilworth in the night, and cut to pieces; while Simon himself, without armour or even clothing, had to flee for shelter to his father's castle which stood close by.

Meanwhile his father made several successful efforts to extricate himself from the blockade he was undergoing on the right bank of the Severn. He crossed the river after several skilful manoeuvres, advanced to Worcester, and then to Evesham, "hourly expecting to form a junction with the forces under his son. On the morning of the 4th of August, 1265, when looking in the direction of his stately castle of Kenilworth, he saw a force descending the hills, their armour glittering in the sun, and bearing his own standards. But he soon discovered that these had been taken from Simon's routed force, and that under them the enemy had stolen upon him, closing around him surely, in front, on flank, and rear. Bewildered by the precision and secresy of this combined movement, the earl, after a gloomy pause, shook his gauntleted hand heavenward, and exclaimed, "They have learned from me the art of war! May God have mercy on our souls, for our bodies are the prince's!"

He now made every effort to array his lesser force in order of battle; after which he spent a short time in prayer, and received the sacrament, as he was always wont to do before fighting.

The battle began about two in the afternoon, and was barely concluded by sunset, so rancorous was the hate on both sides.

The first movement was made by Leicester attempting, at the head of his knights and men-at-arms,'to cut a passage to the Kenilworth road; but he failed in this, being deserted by his Welsh followers in the heat of the onset. Fighting sword in hand, and in front, he strove by every example to withstand the efforts of Prince Edward, who displayed the most brilliant valour on the other side. His friends were falling fast on every hand, and their followers becoming disheartened. All order being lost, he formed them into a solid circle on the summit of an eminence, and by spear and axe repelled for a time the assaults of the Royalists, by whom they were completely surrounded. In one of these old King Henry, whom Leicester had cruelly led into the field to do battle against his own son and his own cause, and whose features were concealed by the bars of a riveted helmet, was unhorsed, thrown to the ground, and in danger of being dispatched (according to Hemingburgh), when he cried to his assailant with a loud voice, "Hold, fellow! I am Henry of Winchester, thy king!" On this he was saved, and Prince Edward, who was close by, on recognising his voice, had him conveyed to a place of safety, and asking his blessing, rushed once more into the conflict.

By this time the small army of Leicester was wavering more than ever. His son Henry had been killed by his side. His horse fell beneath the closing spears, yet, freeing himself from the saddle and the dying animal, the earl fought with the fury that is born of desperation. Seeing all hopeless, he asked of the Royalists if they would give quarter.

"No quarter to traitors!" was the stern shout; and soon after he fell, sword in hand, near the corpse of his gallant son, who had fallen in seeking to defend him. All was over then; defeat and the slaughter of his followers ensued, just as the sun was going down.

All the ferocity that civil strife engenders was exhibited

by the king's party on this occasion; no prisoners were taken, and of Leicester's army there fell in this battle at Evesham 180 barons and knights, and an unnumbered multitude of inferior vassals. The body of the ambitious earl was found among the dead near that of his son. Roger Mortimer hewed off the head, and barbarously sent it to his wife, as a sure token of victory and of vengeance, for she had been ever one of Leicester's greatest enemies. The bodies of father and son were then mutilated after a fashion singularly horrible; and after being dragged to Evesham, were there, together with the remains of the Justiciary, Hugh de l'Espenser, buried in the church belonging to the abbey, the stately tower of which is still remaining.

"No quarter to traitors".

A pedestal still commemorates the site of this battle, which replaced the English crown more firmly on the head of a weak and credulous king, whose lot was cast in stormy times, when a strong and almost tyrant hand was ever needed to hold the helm of the State. During the absence of his son Edward in Palestine he died, worn out by the troubles of a reign, save that of George III, the longest ever known in Britain.

SEA-FIGHT IN THE CHANNEL

Twenty-one years after Edward's accession, there arose a naval war between France and England. In 1286, Edward was the first who appointed a person to the office of Admiral of the English Seas, as we find William de Leybourne styled "Admiral de le Mer du dit Roy d'Angleterre," at an ordinance made at Bruges concerning the conduct of the ships of England and Flanders in that year; and about the same time first mention is made of an admiral of France, named Florent de Varenne, whose successor, Enguerrand, was "Admiral de la Flotte du Roi Philippe le Hardi," yet never was the sea more infested by piracy than in 1293, the period referred to. The feeble execution of the laws had given licence to all kinds of men; and a general appetite for rapine, followed by revenge for it, seemed to infect the mariners and fighting merchant-traders of the time, and tempted them on the smallest provocation to seek redress by immediate and merciless retaliation on the aggressors.

It chanced that a Norman and an English vessel met near the coast of Bayonne (De Mezeray has it Guienne), and both having occasion for water, sent their boats ashore at the same time, and, as misfortune would have it, to the same spring, upon which there immediately ensued a quarrel for precedence. In the squabble a Norman drew his dagger and attempted to stab an English seaman, who grappling with him, hurled him to the ground. The Norman was said to have fallen on his own dagger; be that as it may, the man was slain, and from this petty scuffle between two obscure seamen about a cask of water, there grew a bloody war between two great nations, involving half of Europe in the quarrel. The mariners of the Norman ship laid their complaints before the King of France, who, without caring to inquire into the matter, bade them "take revenge, and trouble him no more about it." Though more legal than usual in applying to the crown, they required but this hint to proceed to immediate outrage.

Meeting an English ship in the Channel, they boarded her, and hanging some of the crew, together with some dogs, from the yard-arms, in presence of their shipmates, bade them inform their countrymen that "vengeance was now taken for the blood of the Norman killed at Bayonne."

This injury, accompanied by circumstances so insulting, was speedily resented by all the mariners of the Cinque Ports, who, without the empty formality of appealing to King Edward, retaliated by committing precisely the same barbarities on all French vessels without distinction; and the French in return preyed upon the ships of Edward's subjects, Gascon as well as English: and soon armed piratical craft of all kinds swarmed in the Channel and Bay of Biscay in pursuit of each other, the sovereigns of both countries remaining perfectly indifferent the while. The English formed private associations with the Irish and Dutch seamen, the French with the Genoese and Flemings; and the animosities of these lawless spirits became more and more violent.

A fleet of 260 Norman vessels set sail to the south for wine, and in their passage seized all the English ships they met, and hanging or drowning the crews, made spoil of the cargoes, and arrived in triumph at St. Mahé, a port in Bretagne. Filled with fresh fury by this incident, the English ports fitted out a fleet of eighty sail, stronger and better manned, to take revenge. Depredations had now been carried to such a length, that at last the nations agreed on a certain day to decide the dispute with their whole naval strength, and a large empty ship was placed in the Channel midway between the coasts of England and France to mark the spot of the engagement.

On the 14th April, 1293, they met in close battle. Long and obstinate was the engagement, and no quarter was either asked for or given; in the end the French were totally routed, and the -greater part of their ships taken, sunk, or destroyed, and "the majority of their crews perished in the ocean." It has been alleged that the loss of the French was 15,000 men. If so, it can only be accounted for by the circumstance that the returning Norman fleet was transporting a considerable body of troops from the south.

Matters were now looking serious; and Philip, enraged by a defeat so murderous and disgraceful, dispatched an envoy to London demanding reparation. He did more, for he cited Edward to appear in his Court of Parliament, as his liege man and vassal, being Duke of Guienne, and having done homage on his knees as such before Philip, at Paris, in 1274. The English king sent his brother; but Philip, dissatisfied with this equivocation, declared him contumacious, and seized his French possessions. On finding himself in something like the same absurd feudal snare he had prepared for the Scots, Edward was exasperated; the more so when he found France making preparations to invade England at a time when his hands were full with his northern neighbours: so, to anticipate any descents on the coast, besides three formidable fleets which were to protect it, he equipped a fourth consisting of above 330 ships, with a body of 7,000 men-at-arms and archers on board, under the command of the Earl of Lancaster, to recover his forfeited duchy of Guienne. He sailed to the mouth of the Garonne, took a town or two, and thence went to Bourdeaux and Bayonne, after the capture of which he died; but all this did not prevent a French fleet of 300 sail, under the command of Matthew de Montmorenci and John de Harcourt, assisted by Thomas de Tuberville, an English traitor, from landing at Dover, and reducing that town to ashes, ere the men of the country rose, and compelled the invaders fly to their ships with considerable loss.

CHAPTER V

STIRLING BRIDGE, 1297 - FALKIRK, 1298

STIRLING BRIDGE

I N DETAILING the preceding sea-fight, we have somewhat anticipated a quarrel the most disastrous perhaps in British history, and which for many generations of men was the cause of bloodshed.

In 1282, Scotland was in all the enjoyment of profound peace, and of most unprecedented prosperity, under the gentle sway of Alexander III, who had married Margaret, a daughter of Henry III of England, and consequently was brother-in-law of the reigning king of that country, Edward I. In the forty-second year of his age, and having a son and daughter grown to maturity, Alexander had every prospect of leaving his sceptre to a long line of descendants. The year 1282 saw his daughter united in marriage to Eric, the young King of Norway; and soon after his son, who was named after himself, married the daughter of Guy of Dampierre, the powerful Count of Flanders.

But a brief space of time sufficed to cover with sorrow and darkness all this prospect of a happy future. The Queen of Norway had only been married a year, when she died in giving birth to a daughter; the death of Prince Alexander, without heirs, followed in January 1284; and on the 16th March, two years afterwards, the king, when riding on a dark night, was thrown from his horse over a high cliff at Kinghorn, opposite Edinburgh, and killed on the spot. By this fatality terminated the male line of the Celtic or old Macalpine kings, who had ruled the race of the Dalriadic Scots from the prehistoric times of dark and unknown antiquity - times clouded by fable and romance - and now the sovereignty of the most turbulent kingdom in Europe devolved upon an infant Norwegian princess, who, of course, was still absent at the court of her father. Had this child survived, the calamities that fell upon her kingdom might perhaps have been averted. The crown of her grandfather had been secured to her by the estates of the realm and since his death it had been arranged that as soon as she was brought home she should be betrothed to her second cousin, the eldest son of the King of England - a measure which, had it been carried out, might have finally united the two kingdoms under one sceptre - but this politic hope was doomed to blight, for on her passage home, the little Queen of Scotland died in the Orkneys, in her eighth year. When tidings of this fatal event came, "the kingdom was troubled," says the Bishop of St. Andrew's, "and its inhabitants sank into despair."

And now there fell on Scotland the greatest and most terrible calamity that can befall a warlike state - a disputed succession - but in this case, advantage was taken by the bold, able, and unscrupulous Edward I to endeavour to make himself master of Scotland by force or fraud; and for more than twenty years the land was involved in all the barbarities of a war, waged as only in those days war was waged, bequeathing to posterity a long and unmeaning inheritance of hate. Thirteen competitors appeared for that crown which has been so often one of thorns for its hapless wearer; but the claims of two, John Baliol and Robert Bruce, were declared by Edward, who was unhappily selected as umpire, superior to the rest. They were the descendants of David, a younger brother of William I, surnamed "The Lion," from having first borne that cognisance on his seals and banners; Baliol being the grandson of the eldest daughter, Bruce the son of the second. Finding Baliol mean, timid, pliant, and ambitious, Edward, intending ere long to advance his own imaginary claim, decided in his favour, a measure which ultimately retarded the union of the countries for centuries. Prior to making any award, Edward, with great cunning and foresight, had required that English garrisons should be put in the principal fortresses, on the plea that the gift might be in the hand of him who was to bestow it.

To the disgust and indignation of the Scots, the half Norman Baliol did fealty to Edward for the crown awarded him, and the spring of 1296 saw the nation in arms against him. This effort, however, was conducted without ability, and after a short time Edward again overran the Lowlands; and as this was called the suppression of a "rebellion," the sword was allowed more than usual licence, and even priests were murdered in cold blood within the rails of the altar, as it was sought by sheer massacre to strike terror into the hearts of the people. On the 2nd of July, the miserable Baliol surrendered into the hands of Edward the kingdom which should never have been his, and which he had obtained on terms unknown to the Scottish people; and an English noble, John de Warrenne, Earl of Surrey, was made governor over it, or at least that part of it where English garrisons lay, with Hugh Cressingham as his Justiciary. Edward's conception, the union of the entire island under one crown, was doubtless a great one; it was infamously and cruelly enforced, but was never to be achieved by the sword.

Amid incessant turmoil, petty strife, and marauding, this state of matters only remained two years, when a body of Scots were again in arms. This time their leader was William Wallace, a man neither rich nor noble, but the second son of Sir Malcolm Wallace, of Ellerslie, near Paisley. He is said by his detractors to have come of Norman blood; but even were it so, the lapse of 230 years and nearly six generations must have made him Scot enough to resent the oppression of his country. His father, his elder brother, and many of his kinsmen, had been slain in skirmishes with the enemy. His wife and family had been burned with his house at Lanark, and from that time he devoted himself to the cause of vengeance and freedom. Distinguished for bravery and hardihood, in an age when all men were hardy and brave, the fond admiration of his countrymen has endued him with attributes of strength and beauty equalled only by the demigods of Homer; but, however, his many achievements prove that he must have been no ordinary man. Scotland owed little then as ever to her unpatriotic and infamous nobility; and in this case it was to one of the people she was to owe all her future existence. ," When we read the story of William Wallace," says an eloquent English writer, "imagination wanders back to the times of heroic antiquity, and enthusiasm can scarcely keep pace with reason in forming an estimate of his services to his country. He gave new birth to the land of his nativity, and interested the sympathies of the world in behalf of her gallant struggle for existence. Personal wrong and the grinding oppression practised on his friends first stung him to revolt; but his passion soon hardened into principle, like the burning lava converted into stone. Against the victorious might of England he threw himself, and carved his way to honour without the shouts of a thousand vassals to proclaim his feudal greatness, or a coronet on his brow to tell of the nobility of his blood. Fortune did not look askance upon his sacrifice. The discipline of English chivalry quailed before him; castles changed masters; ridicule gave way to reflection; the oppressor deigned to assign reasons for his oppression; injury and insult were followed by retaliation and revenge; the haughty Plantagenet found himself no longer invincible; and conquest gained by so many intrigues, so much artful policy, and such elaborate chicane, vanished like a dream."

Among the many victories he won, that at Stirling Bridge, on the 13th of September, 1297, is alike the most splendid and remarkable. Edward I was then warring with France, but he had remitted to John de Warrenne, Earl of Surrey and Sussex, and to Hugh Cressingham (whom we have already named), a military ecclesiastic, his Lieutenant and Treasurer, or Justiciary, in Scotland, full power to repress all resistance; and for this purpose an army of 50,000 infantry and a great body of horse, under their orders, marched through the south Lowlands in quest of Wallace, who was then besieging Dundee with all the men that he and his friends, Graham, Ramsay, and Murray, could muster - only 10,000 in all. Yet, quitting Dundee, they crossed the Tay and marched with all speed to dispute with the English the passage of the Forth, by which they alone could penetrate into the more northern parts of the kingdom.

The bridge across the Forth near Stirling was then of timber, and stood at Kildean, where some remains of the stone pillars which supported the woodwork are still visible, exactly half a mile above the present ancient bridge. It is described as having been so narrow that only two persons could pass along it abreast, yet the English leaders absurdly proposed to make 50,000 foot and all their horse undergo the tedious operation of passing it in the face of an enemy. Walter de Hemingburgh, Canon of Gisborough, in Yorkshire, and author of a History of England from 1066 to 1308, records that a Scottish traitor named Sir Richard Lunday (Lundin?), who served the Earl of Surrey, strenuously opposed this measure, and pointed out a ford at no great distance where sixty men could have crossed the stream abreast; but no regard was paid to his suggestions, and the sequel proved how headstrong was the folly of the English leaders. To increase their troubles, they, had in their army certain Scottish barons of the Baliol faction, on whom, with their followers, they could little rely in case of disaster. Notwithstanding all his force, Surrey was by no means anxious to encounter Wallace, whose success in past encounters had won him a formidable name; he wished to avoid a general action, all the more so that he knew that he was about to be superseded in his post by Brian Fitzalan, and consequently was less zealous in the cause of the king their master.

Seeking therefore to temporise, he dispatched two Dominican friars to Wallace, whose force was then encamped near Cambuskenneth Abbey, on the hill so well known as the Abbey Craig; thus both armies were within perfect view of each other, and only separated by the river, which there winds like a silver snake between the green and fertile meadows. The request of the friars was brief - that Wallace and his followers should lay down their arms and submit...'

"Return to your friends," said he, "and tell them we come here with no peaceful intent, but ready for battle, determined to avenge our wrongs and to set our country free. Let your masters come and attack us; we are ready to meet them beard to beard."

Enraged by this reply, many of the English knights now clamoured to be led on. Then it was that the active traitor

Wallace and the monks.

Lunday said to Surrey, '' Give me but five hundred horse and a few foot, and I shall turn the enemy's flank by the ford, while you, my Lord Earl, may pass the bridge in safety."

Still Surrey hesitated, on which Hugh Cressingham exclaimed, passionately, "Why do we thus protract the war, and waste the king's treasure? Let us fight, it is our bounden duty." Surrey, contrary to his own judgment, yielded; and by dawn of day the English began to cross the bridge, and Wallace heard the tidings with joy. Slow was this process; when the sun rose they were still defiling across, and were permitted to do so without interruption till eleven o'clock, by which time one-half of Surrey's army was over the river, and gradually forming in order of battle, while the Scots looked quietly on from the gentle slope above it.

The reader must bear in mind that, save in the details of their surcoats, banners, and insignia, these two armies, English and Scottish, were now pretty much alike in their war equipment. On one side were the banners of the English, bearing the arms then chosen by Edward I. - gules, three lions passant regardant; St. George argent, a cross gules and of St. Edward the Confessor, a cross fleury between six martlets, or, on the other side floated the Scottish lion rampant, and the silver cross of St. Andrew. Now the tunics worn over the mail-shirts were elaborately painted and blazoned, and those curious ornaments called *ailettes* were worn on the shoulders of knights in battle. The barrel-shaped helmets were surmounted by their crests; that of Wallace was a dragon. Skull-caps, spherical and conical, were worn by the infantry; in lieu of the long pennons, the lances now had little emblazoned banners; the mail gloves of the hauberks were divided into separate fingers; and triangular shields were almost universally worn: for every generation saw some improvement in the panoply for man and horse.

When one-half of the Englishmen were over, Wallace-began

to advance, having previously sent a strong detachment to hold the ford already referred to. The moment the Scots began to move, Sir Marmaduke Twenge, a gallant knight, belonging to the North Riding of Yorkshire, who, together with Cressingham, led the vanguard of horse, displayed the royal standard amid loud cries of "For God and St. George of England!" and at the head of the heavily-mailed horse, made a furious charge up the slope upon the Scottish infantry, who received the shock upon their levelled spears, while their archers kept shooting fast and surely from the rear, and caused the English forces to waver and recoil upon each other.

Led on by Wallace, Sir John Grahame of Dundaff, Ramsay of Dalhousie, and others, the Scots made a furious downhill charge towards the bridge; while in the meantime a masterly movement was executed by another body, who by a quick detour got in between it and those who had already crossed the river, completely cutting off their retreat. All became immediate confusion, 2nd the little discipline then known was entirely lost. Wallace, as soon as he saw the movement for intercepting their retreat achieved, pressed on with greater fury; and the half-formed columns of the English on the north bank of the river began at once to give way, and thousands of their heavy-armed cavalry were hurled into the river and drowned. Surrey, who witnessed this scene from the opposite bank, sought to retrieve the fortune of the day by sending across, at a moment when the bridge was open, a strong reinforcement at full speed, with his own banner; but unable to form amid the recoiling masses of their own infantry, they only added to the confusion and slaughter, being assailed on every side by Scottish spearmen. At this terrible moment the bridge parted, a disaster of which there are several versions; but this catastrophe, together with the passage of the river by a body of Scots at the ford, whence they fell on Surrey's own rear, decided the victory. An incredible number of English were drowned in attempting to cross the stream. There perished the nephew of Sir Marmaduke Twenge, a young knight greatly beloved by his soldiers; while his uncle cut his way across the bridge ere it fell, and escaped. On being advised at first to throw himself into the river, he replied, "It shall never be said of me that I voluntarily drowned myself. God forbid that such dishonour should ever fall on any Englishman!"

The traitor Scottish barons who served in Surrey's ranks - one of whom was the Earl of Lennox - now threw off the mask, and, with their followers, joined in the pursuit, when the flight became, as usual in those days, a mere scene of barbarous slaughter. "No quarter was given. The country for miles round was covered with the bodies of the English soldiers; 20,000 men are believed to have fallen in the battle and the flight. Among these was Cressingham, a man so detested by the Scots that they mangled his dead body, and are said to have torn the skin from the limbs. The loss of the Scots was trifling; and the only man of note among them that fell was Sir Andrew Moray." Surrey, after making one brave attempt to rally his soldiers in the Torwood, on being assailed by Wallace, again resumed his flight, and rode on the spur to Berwick, and thence sent to his master news of his terrible defeat.

Scottish historians assert that the bridge had been sawn through by order of Wallace, and that on a certain trumpet being sounded, a man beneath it drew out a wedge, and let the whole fabric fall. On the other hand, an English chronicler says it was broken down by Surrey to secure his retreat. The present burgh seal of Stirling seems to commemorate this victory. It represents the old wooden bridge, in the centre of which is a crucifix. At the south end are soldiers with English bows attempting to pass, on the northern are others with Scottish spears; and the legend around it is, '*Hie armis Bruti, Scoti stant hie cruce tuti*' a plain allusion to the safety of Church and State resulting from the valour and victory of Sir William Wallace, who by this event also won the castle of Stirling, where he supped that night with his companions. The Scots now regarded him as the deliverer of their country, and crowded to his standard. He was chosen protector of the kingdom, an office which he executed with fidelity and dignity, though not without exciting the malignity of those who have so generally been Scotland's curse, her nobility; and as warfare had brought a famine on the land, and a pestilence too - "produced by the exhalations from the putrid carcasses that lay rotting on the ground, aggravated by the deficient and unhealthy food of the people" - he marched his army into England, that he might subsist it in the northern counties, and send food to the famishing people at home.

By the result of this single battle the English were entirely driven out of Scotland, save at Roxburgh and Berwick, in the castles of which two gallant garrisons maintained a stubborn resistance, till they were relieved by Surrey when, in January, 1298, he entered Scotland for that purpose.

FALKIRK

Filled with rage at the effect produced by the battle at Stirling, and the terrible retaliations of the Scots in the English border counties, Edward concluded in haste a truce with the King of France, and hastened home intent on vengeance. He reached England about the middle of March, and instantly summoned the barons and other military tenants to assemble with their followers at York on the Feast of Pentecost; and he also pompously ordered the Scottish nobles to meet him in the same place on the day appointed, threatening otherwise condign punishment; but to this summons they paid not the slightest regard, either deterred by fear of Wallace, or ashamed at last of their own treason and supineness. But so little reliance had his own peers on the faith

The Battle of Stirling Bridge.

of Edward, that they refused to march against the Scots until he ratified in person the Magna Charta and the Charter of Forests. Unwilling to comply, and yet fearing to evade, with his usual cunning, he induced the Bishop of Durham and three earls to take a solemn oath, '' on the soul of their lord the king," that if he obtained victory he would perform his promise. The suspicious barons were obliged to content them with this, and began their march against the Scots under Wallace; prior to which movement Edward made a pilgrimage to the shrine of St. John of Beverley, whose consecrated banner he is supposed to have brought with him. By his laws, every man was compelled to arm according to his station, that is to say, according to the amount of his property - those who possessed land to the value of £15, and goods to the value of 40 marks, were required to have a hauberk, an iron cap, knife, and horse; those possessed of 40 shillings, a sword, bow, knife, and arrows.

In the month of June he entered Scotland by the eastern borders, the forces being led by himself in person. Under his immediate orders were Anthony de Beck, the famous fighting' Bishop of Durham; Humphrey de Bohun, Earl of Hereford and Essex, and High Constable of England; Bigod, Earl of Norfolk, the Chief Marshal; the Earl of Lincoln; and Radulf, Lord Basset de Drayton, afterwards, in extreme old age, one of the first Knights of the Garter. At Roxburgh he reviewed his army, which consisted of 80,000 infantry, English, Welsh, and Irish, besides a powerful body of splendidly mailed, mounted, and disciplined cavalry, the veterans of his French wars; 3,000 of these rode horses completely armed from head to crupper, and 4,000 were light cavalry. In addition to these were 500 special *gens de cheval* from Gascony, nobly mounted and magnificently accoutred. His whole force mustered more than 90,000 helmets.

He poured these forces through the Lothians, where, after a brave resistance, the great castle of Dirleton, the stronghold of the

73

Scoto-Norman family of De Vaux, was surrendered to Anthony Beck, whose troops suffered from a scarcity of provisions, and were compelled to subsist on the beans and peas in the fields - a circumstance, says Lord Hailes, in his Annals, which presents us with a favourable view of agriculture in Haddingtonshire so far back as the thirteenth century. Without meeting any other obstacle of importance, the great host marched onward till it reached the Priory of the Scottish Knights of the Temple, at Kirkliston, where Edward halted and encamped for a month, waiting for his supplies by sea, as he intended to march into the western counties and crush for ever the rebellion of the Scots, as he curiously termed their resistance of his armed invasion.

Indefatigable and undismayed, Wallace had meanwhile collected from amid the peasantry, of whom he was the guardian, and to whom he was an idol, a resolute force of 30,000 men. With these he marched to Falkirk in West Lothian, where, with great skill and perception, he chose a strong military position, having in its front a morass through which no cavalry could approach, while he covered his flanks by rude field-works of palisades driven into the earth and bound together by ropes. Provisions soon became scarce in Edward's camp at Kirkliston; the fleet from Berwick was anxiously looked for. The surrounding country had been many times wasted by fire and sword; the soldiers complained bitterly of their scanty provender, and a change of quarters to Edinburgh was contemplated. A small supply was procured; but on the great body of the fleet being still detained by adverse winds, a dangerous mutiny broke out in the English army. Under his banner Edward had 40,000 Welsh, led by their chiefs, whom he had but recently subjected to his stern sway. These hardy mountaineers were not over-zealous in his service, and on them the famine was permitted to press hardest. A supply of wine sent to them by Edward brought on a crisis. Whether it was served too liberally is unknown now;

but in a sudden paroxysm of national antipathy, they fell upon the English in their tents at night. Edward's trumpets sounded promptly to horse, and charging the Welsh he slew more than eighty of them, and restored order. Exasperated and sullen, the Welsh chiefs now openly threatened to join Wallace.

"Let them do so," said Edward, scornfully; "let them go over to my enemies. I hope soon to see the day when I shall chastise them both."

It was at this very crisis of the Welsh discontent that Wallace had ably planned a night assault upon the English camp, a movement which if properly executed might have ended, by panic and confusion, in the destruction of Edward's army; but his scheme was frustrated by two of those ignoble peers who, ever since the voice of the people had chosen him guardian of Scotland, had envied his power, as the son of a mere lesser baron, and took every opportunity of resisting his authority. These traitors were Gilbert de Umphraville, Earl of Angus, and Patrick, Earl of Dunbar; who in the dusk secretly sought the King of England, and informed him that "William Wallace, then encamped in a fortified position in the forest of Falkirk, had heard of his proposed retreat, and intended to surprise him by a night attack, and to hang upon and harass his rear."

"Thanks be to God, who hath hitherto extricated me from every peril!" exclaimed Edward, with stern triumph; "they shall not need to follow me, these Scots, since I shall go forth to meet them."

Accordingly, at three o'clock in the afternoon of the 20th July, he put his cavalry and infantry in motion, and marching to Linlithgow, encamped on the Burgh Muir, to the eastward of that town. The Tear-guard, with the pavilions and sumpter horses, not having come up, the troops lay for that night on the bare heath, the cavalry having no other forage than the furze and grass of the moor. Though a tyrant, and merciless to his enemies, Edward of England was every inch a soldier; so that night he slept in his armour, by his horse's side, with his sword and shield for a pillow.

Startled by some distant sound about midnight, the barbed charger trod heavily upon its royal master, and crushing his shirt of mail - perhaps the identical suit that is now preserved in the Tower of London - broke three of his ribs. Edward's cry of agony, and the trampling of hoofs, caused a panic in the bivouac, and there arose on all sides cries of "Treason! Treason! The king is wounded; the Scots are upon us!"

But the dawn of the midsummer morning soon brightened on Torduff and the Pentland peaks. Edward mounted, and showing himself to his troops, dispelled their fears, after the bruises had been dressed by his surgeon, Monsieur Philip de Belvey. He then ordered his banners to be unfurled, the trumpets to sound, and once more his vast army resumed its march towards the forest of Falkirk, where the little town of that name, with its ancient church of St. Modan, rose on high and commanding ground.

As the English approached the hills of Muiravonside the flashing of steel was seen in front. These were the helmets and lances of some Scottish horse thrown forward by Wallace to reconnoitre, as Hemingburgh records, and they soon fell back on his main body. On gaining the summit of the heights of Maddiston and those south of Callender Wood, the whole English army halted, while mass was celebrated by the Bishop of Durham, Anthony de Beck, Patriarch of Jerusalem, and Lord of the Isle of Man, in full armour, with a sword by his side, and a shield slung at his back. Then, as now, the view which met the eyes of that English host from the heights of Callender was one of wonderful beauty. At their feet lay the fertile carse of Falkirk, and the vast oak forest known as the Tor-wood stretching away to where the towers and town of Stirling rose in the sunshine.

The river Forth flowed between, like a thread of blue and silver between forests of natural wood in all the foliage of summer. In the background were the peaks of the Ochils - part of the dark and distant Grampians - that rose Alp on Alp, a barrier between the Lowlander and Celt; and in the immediate foreground, midway between Falkirk and the river of Carron, was the army of the' Scottish patriot, their 36,000 helmets shining in the sun.

William Wallace.

This was on St. Magdalen's day, the 22nd of July.

Edward, who was as politic as he was brave, proposed to refresh his soldiers; but, confident in their overwhelming numbers, they clamoured to be led against the Scots. Edward consented, "in the name of the Holy Trinity," and the English advanced in three columns, each of 30,000 men.

The first was led by the Earl Marshal, having under his orders the Earls of Hereford and Lincoln; the second was led by the fighting Bishop of Durham, having under his orders Radulf Basset de Drayton, for a time English governor of Edinburgh Castle; and the third was led by Edward in person.

Wallace had drawn up the Scots in three *schiltrons*, or columns of less than 10,000 men each. These were almost entirely composed of peasantry; for, being keenly jealous of his increasing popularity, few knights and still fewer barons would join him. Under him, however, there served as leaders Sir John Stewart of Bonhill, who commanded the archers of Ettrick Forest, and the hardy Brandanes of Bute, or vassals of the Great Steward, of whom 1,200 were in the field; Sir John, the Graham of Abercorn and Dundaff, wearing the sword which his dying father had bequeathed to him on the fatal field of Dunbar; Duncan Macduff, eleventh Earl of Fife, a youth of twenty years of age; and John Comyn, son of the Lord of Badenoch. The three last-named led each a column drawn up in the ancient form of an orb, with the spearmen in front, having their long weapons levelled from the hip to repel cavalry. The immediate front ranks knelt on the right knee, against which the butt of the spear was planted, exactly as in the present mode of preparing to receive a charge of horse; and the circle was the simple old Scottish order of battle prior to the introduction of -the solid square.

In his chronicle, Langtoft says that the Scots stood like a "castelle, the spears poynt over poynt" Between each of these *schiltrons* was placed a band of border archers; while 1,000 well-armed and well-mounted horsemen - all the Scottish chief could muster - formed a corp-de-reserve under John Comyn, and remained in the rear for any emergency.

While the Bishop of Durham had been celebrating mass on the hill, the same solemn sacrament was performed, amid equal silence and awe, in the Scottish ranks; and all awaited steadily the advance of the foe. Hitherto the leaders of these unfortunate men had acted with pretended unanimity; but now, at this most critical moment, a dispute arose about the chief command. Sir John Stewart, as the representative of his brother, the hereditary Lord High Steward, claimed it; the traitor Comyn boasted of his descent from King Donald; while the more modest Wallace asserted that with him lay the right to lead, as the legally authorised guardian of the country. But Sir John Stewart upbraided him as one who aspired to a dignity far above his rank; and tauntingly compared him to "the owl in the fable, which, having dressed itself with borrowed feathers, affected not only a beauty above its kind, but a dominion over the whole winged tribe."

The foe was still advancing, and still the dispute continued; but, sensible of the peril that menaced all, Wallace maintained his temper and with it his authority.

Led by the Earl Marshal, by Lincoln, and Hereford, the first column came furiously on; but not having reconnoitred the ground, their leading files rolled pell-mell into the morass, where horse and man, English and Gascon alike, were exposed to the arrows of the Scottish archers. Swerving a little to the left, however, they found firmer ground, and closing their files, charged.

"Now," exclaimed Wallace, with pleasant confidence, to his soldiers, "I haif brocht ye to the ring hop gif ye can!" and at that moment the heavily-mailed English cavalry of the first line fell with a tremendous shock on the charged spears of his right flank, while sharp and sure - for there was then no smoke of arquebuse or musket to impede an aim - the archers of Bonhill plied their shafts obliquely among them. Perceiving the mistake made by the first column, the second, under the Bishop of Durham, avoided the morass, and wheeling to the right menaced the Scottish left; but so steady was its aspect that the warlike prelate, though his men were three to one, proposed a halt until the king came up with the reserves. On this Radulf Basset exclaimed, scornfully, "Stick to thy mass, thou Lord Bishop; we shall conduct the military operations of the day!"

"On, then; for this day we are all bound to do our duty as good soldiers," replied the bishop. And brandishing his sword, he led on his column, amid the glittering lances of which there floated no less than thirty-six banners of the noblest families in England, and fell thundering on the Scottish left, while the Earl Marshal assailed their right. At that very moment, to the astonishment of the English and the bewilderment of Wallace, Comyn drew off, some allege, 10,000 of his vassals, and with the utmost deliberation quitted the field. "That there was treachery among the Scottish nobles," says Tytler, "is satisfactorily proved by Hemingburgh, an English historian, who says that the Scottish horse fled without striking a blow (*absque ullo gladii ictu*) when the battle had just begun. The Scottish cavalry was a body of 1,000 horse, amongst whom were the flower of the Scottish knights and barons. Are we to believe that these, from mere timidity, fled before a lance was put in rest, and upon the first look of the English?" Another writer alleges that "it sprang from the treachery of Comyn, who led them, and their-infatuated jealousy of the Scottish guardian. Undismayed, his followers, though now but 20,000 opposed to more than 90,000, stood firm; and Wallace did all that a brave man could do to inspire them, fighting in front with his two-handed sword - his stature, conspicuous position, and armour, rendering him the mark of many a levelled lance and bended bow."

Again and again the cavalry of the Earl Marshal and De Beck spurred in furious charges on the Scottish pikes. Stoutly they stood, shoulder to shoulder; and though infantry came up, and showers of cloth-yard shafts were shot point-blank into the ranks of Wallace, while with a storm of stones, the Welsh and Irish slingers plied their missiles securely from behind, they could not penetrate what an .old historian calls "that wood of spears." As if to make up for his recent contumacy, the young Knight of Bonhill, who led the foresters of Ettrick, fought like a hero of romance, but was mortally wounded while in the act of giving orders, and, rolling from his horse, was instantly slain.

The Bishop of Durham's charge at Falkirk.

The archers of Ettrick tried to save him, but in vain; there they all perished to a man: and their tall, athletic, and handsome figures drew forth even the praise of their enemies - at least so says Hemingburgh of Gisborough. Sir John the Grahame, of Dundaff, the friend and *richt-hand* of Wallace, and the young Earl of Fife, with nearly all their vassals, were slain; and now the survivors, disheartened alike by the fall of their three principal leaders, began to lose heart, and fell into disorder. Deserted by their cavalry, and, after the destruction of their archers, left exposed to a pitiless storm of missiles from the English bows and slings, the Scottish infantry, with their long spears levelled over a breastwork of their own dead and dying, made a desperate attempt only to keep their ground; but their numbers were thinning fast and becoming unsteady: and when the English cavalry once more dashed among them, with lance and sword, axe and mace, all was over.

Armed with that great two-handed sword which his fond countrymen superstitiously believed to have been a gift to him from St. Andrew of Bethsaida, the patron of Scotland, long and bravely did Wallace maintain the field; and not until the sun was sinking beyond the western hills did he begin his perilous retreat' by crossing the Carron, near the old Roman ruin then known as Arthur's Oven, where there was a ford when the tide was low. There, at a place called Brian's Ford, near the Carron Iron Works, fell the only Englishman of distinction whom Edward lost, Sir Brian le Jay, Master of the Templars, who, pressing in pursuit, was there unhorsed and slain by the hand of Wallace, whose horse, covered with wounds and stuck full of spearheads and arrows, was only able to bear him across the river, when it sank beneath him and died. He then continued his flight on foot towards Perth, accompanied by 300 chosen men.

Though most of the details of this battle are very minute, authorities vary very strangely in the number of the Scottish slain.

Lingard, after Trivet, computes them at from 20,000 to 30,000; Matthew of Westminster and Harding at 40,000; Hemingburgh at 50,000; and Walsingham at 60,000, twice the number of Scots in the field. The more probable number, as given by others, is about 15,000 men. Edward's loss was very trivial.

The tombs of Sir John Grahame and Sir John Stewart are still preserved at Falkirk; the inscriptions on both have been frequently renewed. No other mementoes of the field remain save a rude block in Callender Wood known as Wallace's Stone, and a tract of ground called Wallace's Ridge.

On Edward's return to London victorious, the citizens received him with triumph; but the fraternity of Fishmongers outshone all their compatriots. "With solemn procession," says Stow, "they passed through the citie, having amongst other pageants and shows, four sturgeons gilted, carried on four horses, and after five-and-forty knights armed, riding on horses made like luces of the sea; and then St. Magnus, with 1,000 horsemen. This they did on St. Magnus' day, in honour of the king's great victory and safe return."

Again the Lowlands were overrun, and castles were retaken and garrisoned by Edward; and history tells how, after totally failing to corrupt and attach Wallace to his own cause, he had him betrayed by a friend, and barbarously executed, in his thirty-fifth year. But, as if to prove how irrepressible is the spirit of freedom, the scaffold on which Wallace died proved the foundation-stone of Scottish independence.

Two years subsequent to that event saw the Scots in arms under Robert Bruce and the spirit of resistance taking deeper root than ever.

BANNOCKBURN, 1314

B Y SEA as well as by land were the Scots tormented at this time by the adherents and subjects of the King of England. To further the war against Scotland, we find that about the year 1300 a fleet of thirty ships, called galleys, barges, snakes, cogs, and boats, was fitted out by the Cinque Ports chiefly. Each of these craft had from twenty to forty men on board, and the whole was commanded by an admiral named Gervase Alard, who had a chaplain, Sir Robert of Sandwich, to confess the sailors. The most of these vessels were named after saints, and every commander was entitled to carry a banner and light. In 1310 the king desired the Chamberlain of North Wales to deliver two anchors and two cables in his care to "Sir Simon de Montacute, whom he had appointed admiral of his fleet going towards Scotland." On the 12th October in the following year, the king commends the zeal and valour of the captain of his fleet off the west coast of Scotland, Sir John of Argyle, whose name is now quite unknown to the Scots. He was styled "Captain and Admiral of the King's fleet in the Isles of Scotland and Argyle;" and on the 25th of March, 1314 brought over in his squadron 4,000 Irish infantry to take part in the ensuing campaign. This personage, say Sir Harris Nicholas, "appears to have been one of those base Scotsmen who adhered to the invader of their country during its struggle for independence. He was in the service of Edward I in 1297, when he was commanded to proceed with horse and arms abroad. On the 13th December, 1307, he and many of his faithless countrymen were enjoined to maintain tranquillity in Scotland during the king's absence in France; and the various duties entrusted to him prove that he possessed the entire confidence of Edward II." In 1310 he was admiral of the fleet serving off the Scottish coast; and lands belonging to the Templars, in Yorkshire, were bestowed upon him as the reward of his treason. Sir John of Argyle died at Ospring, in Kent, in 1316, while on a pilgrimage to Canterbury, leaving a son, also named mysteriously Sir Alan of Argyle.

Whatever efforts the second Edward made by sea or land, they were doomed to be crushed by the memorable battle which was fought at Bannock-burn on Monday, the 24th of June, 1314, and which secured for ever the independence of the Scottish crown, seating the great King Robert firmly on the throne - a battle that was the greatest of his triumphs and the reward of his valour, skill, and undying perseverance.

To prosecute the troublesome war his father had bequeathed him, young Edward, in addition to his own resources, borrowed large sums from the more wealthy monasteries to defray the expenses of a new expedition; and in the spring of 1314 he assembled an army that numbered fully 100,000 men upon the borders. With it there followed a vast multitude of attendants, in the hope of getting plunder. This prodigious host was composed not only of the crown vassals in England, Ireland, and Wales, but of numbers of foreign troops from Flanders, Gascony, Guienne and Aquitaine, Poictou and Languedoc, &c. Eth O'Connor, Prince of Connaught, and twenty-five other Irish chiefs, were summoned to his assistance, and the whole were to muster at Berwick on the 11th of June. Some idea may be formed of the extent of his preparations from the summonses still preserved as issued to the Sheriffs of Durham, Northumberland, Leicestershire, Cheshire and Lancashire, Derbyshire, Lincolnshire, Shropshire, Nottingham, Stafford, and Warwickshire; to the Earls of Hereford, Hertford, Essex, and Gloucester; and to seven barons, requiring them to equip certain quotas of infantry, amounting in all to 26,540 men. In his ranks were 50,000 archers and 40,000 cavalry, of whom

3,000 were completely sheathed in mail, both horse and man. The Welsh auxiliaries were under Sir Maurice de Berkeley, and Edward relied much on them as mountaineers who might cope with the Scots. "But this policy," says Sir Walter Scott, "was not without its risks. Previous to the battle of Falkirk, the Welsh quarrelled with the English men-at-arms, and the feud between them at so dangerous and critical a juncture was reconciled with difficulty. Edward II followed his father's example in this particular, with no better success. They could not be brought to exert themselves in the cause of their conquerors; but they had an indifferent reward for their forbearance. Without arms, and clad only in scanty dresses of linen cloth, they appeared naked in the eyes of the Scottish peasantry; and after the rout at Bannockburn, were massacred by them in great numbers as they retired in confusion towards their own country."

Great care was taken that an abundant supply of provisions should be collected, together with wagons and cars for the conveyance of tents and baggage. Barbour mentions particularly 160 carts laden with poultry alone; and William of Malmesbury says that the multitude of carriages was so great that, if placed in one line, they would have extended sixty miles in length.

Bruce was now master of all Scotland save the castle of Stirling, the blockade of which he had committed to his brother Edward, who concluded a treaty with the English governor, Sir Philip Mowbray, to the effect that the fortress should be surrendered, if not relieved before the festival of St. John the Baptist, which is celebrated on the 24th of June. King Robert was displeased with his brother for the impolicy of a treaty which permitted the King of England to advance with his collected forces, and compelled him to hazard a battle or raise a siege with dishonour.

"What matter is it?" replied Edward Bruce, stoutly." Let all England come, and we shall fight them were they more!"

So King Robert agreed to the treaty, and prepared to meet the English on the appointed day. He had collected his forces in the forest called the Torwood, midway between Stirling and Falkirk, to the number of only 30,000 men, and these were followed by about 20,000 more camp-followers, gillies, women, and children.

Impoverished as the country was by long war, the great deficiency of the Scotch army was cavalry, which, both in numbers and accoutrements, were totally unfit to cope with the English men-at-arms, though it was not every Englishman in those days that could afford body-armour; for the 130 English knights who proposed to assist Dermot of Leinster in recovering his kingdom possessed only sixty coats of mail among them. Bruce knew, both from his own experience and that of Wallace, that a body of Scottish infantry, armed with their long spears, and judiciously posted, could effectively resist all charges of cavalry; and he was not ignorant of the discomfiture of the

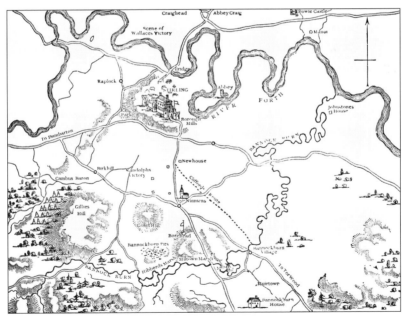

Plan of the battle-field of Bannockburn.

French mounted men-at-arms, under the Constable and the Count of Artois, by the Flemish pikemen at Courtray, in 1304. He resolved, therefore, to fight the battle with his infantry; and "having reviewed his army, he was greatly delighted with the courageous appearance both of the leaders and common soldiers, and addressed them in a cheerful and encouraging manner, urging them to fight manfully in the coming battle, in defence of their lives, fortunes, and liberties, and the honour of his crown."

The Highland clans, which had hitherto held aloof, or looked with grim disdain on the Lowland Scots - the Scoto-Normans and Anglo-Saxons - cutting each other's throats, viewing all as strangers and intruders alike, had now come down from their mountains and joined Bruce in some strength. Among these were twenty-one chiefs - viz., William, third Earl of Sutherland; Angus Macdonald, Lord of the Isles; Sir Malcolm Drummond, ancestor of the Dukes of Perth; Sir Neil Campbell, of Lochow and of Argyle; Sir John Grant, of Grant, who had been a prisoner of war in London in 1297; Sir Simon Fraser, of Oliver Castle, ancestor of the Lords of Lovat; Mackay, Macpherson, Cameron, Sinclair of Roslin, Ross, Macgregor, Mackenzie, and eight others; and, singular to say, the heirs of eighteen of these are still in possession of their estates. Three other chiefs, with their tribes - Macdougal, Cumming,and Macnab - were in the ranks of the English. The place selected by Bruce for the battle, and to bar the approach of the English to Stirling, was a piece of ground then known as the New Park, partly open and partly encumbered with trees; on one side it was protected by a morass, known as the New-miln Bog, the passage of which he knew to be dangerous and difficult. He formed his troops in four columns, apart from each other, yet sufficiently near to keep up communication. Three of these formed a front line facing the south-east, the direction by which the enemy must approach, and extending from the brook or "burn "called the Bannock to the village of St. Ninian. The right wing he protected by means of pits - the suggestion of Sir Malcolm Drummond - dug where the ground was firm, a foot in breadth and three in depth, with a stake in each, and covered lightly with sods and branches. Elsewhere were strewn iron calthrops - pieces of iron all disposed in a triangular form, so that while three of the pikes rest on the ground, a fourth stands in a perpendicular direction, and is especially calculated to lame horses.

On the 22nd, Bruce received tidings that the English were advancing from Edinburgh, and he immediately marched his forces from the Torwood to the positions he had assigned them two days before. The right wing was commanded by his brother Edward; the left was led by Douglas and the young Steward of Scotland; the centre by Thomas Randolph, the veteran Earl of Moray.

The reserve, or fourth column, was led by Bruce in person, Angus of the Isles, his faithful friend and ally, was with him; and there was stationed his little body of cavalry, under Sir Robert Keith, the Mareschal of Scotland, to whom he assigned the particular duty of attacking and, if possible, dispersing the English archers. The royal standard was fixed in the stone which now marks the centre of the Scottish line, and is protected by an iron grating. In Bruce's rear lay a little valley. Above it rose a long, green ridge, now known as the Gillies' Hill, for thereon were all the camp-followers and baggage of his army. The airs to which the Scots are said by history and tradition to have marched to the field are now known as "Bruce's Address" and "The Land of the Leal," a common Dead March with all Scottish regiments; but their instruments could have been only the bagpipe, harp, and kettle-drum.

On the morning of the 23rd of June, the whole army heard mass, which was performed on the field by the aged and blind

Maurice, Abbot of Inchaffray; and perhaps no grander sight can be imagined than the appearance of those 30,000 men, all ready to die for their country, on their knees before God in prayer. Then Bruce caused proclamation to be made that if any man was unprepared to fight and fall with honour, he might depart; but a wild shout responded, and no man quitted his ranks.

On the morning of St. John the Baptist, the 24th of June, the mighty and magnificent array of the English army, with all their spears and banners, was seen debouching from the vast wood which then stretched away towards Falkirk. The June sunshine fell brightly on their burnished arms. According to Barbour, they seemed to cover all the country far and wide, and the mail of the men-at-arms "made the land seem all aglow." Innumerable white banners were waving in the wind, and the particoloured pennons of the knights floated above the glittering columns like a sea. The vanguard of the English, consisting of archers, billmen, and spearmen - comprehending most of the infantry - was now advancing fast, under the Earls of Gloucester and Hereford, who were covered by a heavy body of mailed cavalry as supports. All the remainder of the English troops were so hampered by the narrowness of the ground over which they were compelled by its nature to pass, that then-formation of nine great columns seemed to the eyes of the Scots to form but one enormous mass, gleaming with flashes of armour, and shaded by the multitude of silken banners and pennons that floated over them in the soft summer wind. Edward in person commanded this vast array, surrounded by 400 chosen men, the very flower of his splendid chivalry. Immediately by his side rode Sir Aymer de Valence, who had defeated Bruce at Methven Wood, but was now to see a very different day; Sir Giles de Argentine, a Knight of St. John of Jerusalem, who had covered himself with glory in Palestine, and was accounted "one of the best knights that ever lived;"

and Sir Ingram Umfraville (or Umphraville), a Scottish traitor, but a man of undoubted bravery.

Once again the Scots, when they saw this mighty host rolling towards them like a human sea, joined in a universal appeal to Heaven for aid against the strength of their enemies; an 1, barefooted and bareheaded, the Abbot of Inchaffray passed along the line, with a crucifix in his hand, bestowing benediction and absolution on all sides, while the soldiers knelt before him.

The traitor Umfraville suggested to Edward the policy of feigning a retreat, to lure Bruce from his strong position; but his council was heard with disdain, and on observing the Scots on their knees, "They crave mercy!" exclaimed Edward, joyously. "It is of Heaven, and not your Highness," replied Umfraville; "for on that field they will be victorious or die."

Edward then commanded his trumpets to sound and an attack to be made, and about this time two striking episodes occurred. Previous to the appearance of the English army, on the 23rd, they had detached 800 horse under Sir Robert Clifford, with the double object of reaching Stirling Castle, and of thus releasing from his promise Sir Robert Mowbray, who might then, without dishonour, have made a sortie on the Scottish left wing. They made a great circuit by the low grounds bordering on the Forth, and had actually passed the Scottish left before the eagle eye of Bruce detected the glitter of spears, the flashing of armour, and a long line of dust rolling northward in the direction of Stirling.

"See, Randolph," he exclaimed, "there is a rose fallen from your chaplet! Thoughtless man! you have permitted the enemy to pass."

On this, Randolph hastened at the head of 500 spearmen to repair his fault, for such he deemed it. As he advanced into the plain, Clifford, interrupted in his progress towards Stirling, wheeled his horse to the left and at full speed attacked the party of Scots, who received his charge in close column. Before this wall of spears, Sir William d'Eynecourt, a distinguished knight, was unhorsed and slain. The English cavalry surrounded the little column, and charged it so furiously on every side that Sir James Douglas prayed the king's permission to succour his old comrade, Randolph.

"You shall not stir a foot to help him," replied Bruce; "neither shall I alter my order of battle or lose the advantage of my position. Let him repair his error as he may."

"In sooth I cannot stand by and see Randolph perish," urged Douglas; "therefore, with your leave, I must aid him." Bruce unwillingly consented; but on Sir James hastening to the assistance of his friend, he found the English detachment in complete disorder, and many horses galloping away with empty saddles. On perceiving this, "Halt," cried Douglas; "these brave men have already repulsed the enemy, let us not diminish their glory by seeking to share it."

While this affair took place, the English vanguard was still steadily advancing, but yet so distant that Bruce, who had not yet mounted his battle-charger, was still riding along his line mounted on a small hackney, to see that all were in their places. He carried a battle-axe in his hand, and wore a golden crown upon his helmet, which thus rendered him conspicuous alike to friend and foe as the king. At that moment there came galloping forward from the English vanguard, "a wycht knicht and hardy," named Sir Henry de Bohun, who bravely conceived the idea of terminating the strife at once and covering himself with honour. Couching his lance, he rode furiously at the king.

Armed on all points and more heavily mounted, the encounter would have been most unequal, yet Bruce did not decline it, and rode forward to meet him in his full career. Just as they were about to close he swerved his hackney round, and as De Bohun's lance passed harmless, he clove his head and helmet in twain by one blow of his battle-axe, and laid him dead at his feet. The weapon was shivered by the violence of the stroke; and to those who blamed him for his temerity, he replied simply, "I have broken my good battle-axe."

Led by Gloucester and Hereford, the English vanguard dashed with great bravery at the right wing of the Scots, under Edward Bruce. A rivalry between these two earls made their attack so precipitate as to diminish its effect. Firm stood the Scottish spearmen in their ranks, presenting a serried wall of steel which bore back the enemy. According to Barbour, there was a great crash of spears at the first shock; it could be heard at some distance, and many good knights were dismounted and slain, while their horses, stabbed and maddened with wounds, carried confusion to the rear. When the Earl of Moray saw the right wing thus successfully engaged, he brought up the centre to meet the main body of the English with such spirit that he began to gain ground upon them and to pierce their masses at push of spear, "so that his men appeared to be lost amid the multitude, as if they had been plunged into the sea."

The death of Bohum.

Now came on the Scottish left wing, under Walter, the Great Steward, and Sir James Douglas, so that the whole line was soon engaged in a wild and desperate hand-to-hand conflict with the enemy; and the ground on which they fought was fast becoming one crimson swamp.

Again and again the splendid English cavalry strove by desperate charges to break the columns of Scottish spears, but every attack was repelled, horse and man went down before them; but now those archers, ever so fatal to the Scots, were coming on, and their shafts were beginning to make deadly gaps in the hitherto steady ranks. Their effect had already by sad experience been foreseen, and their attack had been prepared for by Bruce; so Sir Robert Keith, with only 500 chosen mounted men-at-arms, came swiftly round the flank of the morass, and as the multitude of archers had neither pikes or other long weapons wherewith to defend themselves against cavalry, they were almost immediately overthrown, huddled together, cut down, or dispersed in all directions, thus spreading confusion and disorder throughout the whole English army. Part fled to their main body and could not be induced to rally; while now the Scottish bowmen, inferior in number and in skill to their English opponents, came into action, and, after galling the cavalry without opposition, made havoc among them with the short but heavy axes which Bruce had ordered them to wear.

"It was awful," says Barbour, at this crisis, "to hear the noise of these four battles (i.e., columns) fighting in a line; (when Bruce brought his reserve into action) the din of the blows, the clang of arms the shouting of war-cries; to see the flight of arrows, horses running masterless, the alternate rising and sinking of the banners, the ground streaming with blood, and covered with shreds of armour, broken spears, pennons and rich scarfs torn and soiled with blood and clay, and to listen to the groans of the wounded and the dying."

The Scots were still gaining ground, and were pressing on the already wavering masses of the English, shouting from wing to wing, "On them! On them! They fail - they fail!" when at that most critical moment, and while the fortune of that day which was to live for ever in history yet hung in the balance, the Scottish camp-followers on the hill in rear of the reserve, prompted either by enthusiasm or a desire for plunder, suddenly came in sight, with such arms as they could collect, and with sheets and horsecloths displayed on poles as ensigns. This unexpected sight spread instant dismay among the already disheartened ranks of the English, and their whole line began to give way. The eagle eye of Bruce perceived the movement. He put himself at the head of the reserve, and raising his war-cry, fell with redoubled fury on the recoiling enemy, who now gave way in all directions, and then the slaughter became terrible.

The deep ravine of Bannockbum, to the south of the field, lying in the direction taken by most of the fugitives, was literally choked and bridged over by the slain, the difficult nature of the- ground retarding the fugitive horsemen till the. Scottish spears were upon them. Others in great number rushed into the river Forth, and were there drowned miserably. In an attempt to renew the fight, the young Earl of Gloucester rode madly back upon the Scottish infantry, but was immediately unhorsed and slain, at a place still call the Bloody Faulds, though the Scots would gladly have saved his life; but on that day he wore no surcoat above his armour. Seeing all lost, the Earl of Pembroke and Sir Giles de Argentine seized the bridle of Edward, whose courage was undoubted, and forced him off the field. As soon as he was safe, Sir Giles bade him farewell; and adding, "It is not my wont to fly," he raised his war-cry of "Argentine!" and rushing , back upon the Scottish spears was slain, sorrow of King Robert, who knew him well. Argentine was then deemed the flower of English knighthood, and had but lately returned from Palestine and the wars of Henry of Luxembourg. Sir Robert Clifford, renowned in the Scottish wars, and Sir Edward Mauley, Seneschal of England, were also killed; 200 knights and 700 esquires of high birth and blood, inheritors of the noblest names in England, with more than 30,000 of the common file, filled up the roll of slaughter.

Leaving his mighty host to its fate, Edward in his confusion, after making a great circuit, rode to Stirling, where he sought admittance to the castle; but De Mowbray was true to his pledge, and refused to open the gates. The unfortunate king was then compelled to take the road for England, pursued by Sir James Douglas on the spur, with sixty horse. At length the worn fugitive reached the castle of Dunbar, where he was hospitably received by the traitorous Earl of March, who sent him in a fishing skiff to Berwick, "leaving behind him the finest army a King of England ever commanded."

The Scottish loss was very small; Sir William Vipont and Sir Walter Ross were the only persons of consideration who fell. A list of the English lords and knights killed or taken will be found in Trivet's Annals, and the quantity of spoil gained by the victors was inestimable; while the ransoms for life and liberty paid by the prisoners added to the treasury of the long-impoverished Scots.

The Earl of Hereford with a few others fled to Bothwell, where they possessed themselves of the castle; but had soon to surrender.

The castle of Stirling capitulated on the day after the battle. Barbour records that two hundred pairs of gilded spurs were found on the English dead; many of whom lay long unburied, .especially at a place called Polmaise, which signifies "the pool of rotting." Among the prisoners was taken Roger de Northburge, Keeper of the Privy Seal, with the seal itself, which Bruce sent to Edward, on condition that it should never more be used. Scottish historians narrate the great stores found in the English camp, the vessels of gold and silver, the splendid armour, rich apparel, sumptuous horse and tent furniture, and, though last not least, the chest of money for paying the troops.

"O day of vengeance and misfortune!"" exclaimed William of Malmesbury; "odious and accursed day! Unworthy to be included in the circle of the year, which tarnished the glory of England, and enriched the Scots with the plunder of the precious stuffs of our nation to the extent of two hundred thousand pounds (about two millions of our present money); how many illustrious nobles and valiant youths, what numbers of excellent horses and beautiful arms, precious vestments and golden vessels, were carried off in one cruel day!"

King Robert sent the body of the young Earl of Gloucester home; Clifford, Argentine, and others, he interred with the honour due to their rank - the latter in the church of St. Giles at Edinburgh. Sir Marmaduke Twenge, who handed his sword to Bruce, was released and sent home without ransom.

Edward repulsed from Stirling Castle.

Such was the memorable battle of Bannockburn, which, both in its immediate consequences and its more remote effects, even to the present hour, must be regarded as one of the most important events in the annals of our country. It ended for ever the English schemes of conquest; it taught the Scots never to despair "so long as one hundred of them remained alive." Their cities had been sacked, their archives destroyed, their noblest and best had been given to the axe and the gibbet without mercy; all these horrors were over now, and the throne of Scotland was established on as solid and permanent a basis as it had been left by Alexander III. "Dark times indeed succeeded these brilliant days," says Sir Walter Scott, "and none more gloomy than those during the reign of the conqueror's son. But there could be no fear or doubt, there could be no thought of despair, when Scotsmen were hanging, like hallowed reliques, above their domestic hearths the swords with which their fathers served the Bruce at Bannockburn."

Relics of the field are rarely found now, but some of the pits dug by Bruce were opened lately. These were found to have been eighteen inches deep, very close together, with a sharp-pointed stake in each. The stakes were in a state of decomposition, and offered no resistance to the spade; but the bark was sufficiently entire to show that they were of hazel. Some fragments of swords, spear-heads, horseshoes, and horse-hair (the latter mixed with whitish matter like tallow), were found in them. In allusion to the suggestion of Sir Malcolm Drummond, that these pits and the calthrops should be adopted to protect the Scottish position, the armorial supporters of the Drummond family to this day are two naked men bearing clubs, standing on ground studded with spikes; and their significant motto is, "Gang warily."

HALIDON HILL, 1333 - SLUYS, 1346

HALIDON HILL

THE CAUSES which led to "the next great contest between England and Scotland were as follow: - The wise and valiant Bruce, who had won his throne by his sword, and confirmed its independence by a written treaty, was now in his" grave at Dunfermline; and his son, David II, a minor, was left under the care of his old comrade in arms, Randolph, Earl of Moray, as regent of the realm. About this time Edward Baliol, son of John, the whilom puppet King of Scotland, was discovered in a French prison by the Lord Beaumont, an English baron, who claimed the Scottish earldom of Buchan in right of his wife Alicia, daughter of John Comyn, the fourth earl, who had been Constable of Scotland; and deeming young Baliol a suitable instrument for his purpose, he induced him to revive his claim to the Scottish crown. Many other English nobles were in the same situation with Beaumont, having obtained grants of imaginary estates in Scotland, and many nobles of the latter country had lost theirs by adherence to the invaders; so all these saw the utility of Baliol, in stirring up a new war nearly twenty years after Bannockburn. They applied to Edward for his concurrence; but though he wished the enterprise well, he was ashamed to avow his approval of it. He was afraid that injustice would be imputed to him if he attacked with superior force a minor king - a boy and a brother-in-law - whose independent title had been so lately confirmed by solemn treaty and after such terrible bloodshed; but he secretly encouraged Baliol in his lawless claim, connived at the muster of his forces in the north, and gave countenance to all who were disposed to join him: and with only 3,000 men this adventurer landed on the coast of Fife, and marching into the heart of the country, defeated the Earl of Mar, of whose force 12,000 are alleged to have been slain. Baliol now made himself master of Perth, and at Scone was crowned by his followers as "King of Scotland." But he lost his imaginary power almost as quickly as he won it; being unexpectedly attacked near Annan by Sir Archibald Douglas and other loyal chieftains, who routed him, slew his brother John, and chased him in a wretched plight home to England. In this extremity, the servile but ambitious Baliol had again recourse to Edward III, without whose assistance he saw that his designs on the Scottish crown were vain. He offered, if it were obtained for him, to do homage for it, to acknowledge Edward's superiority over it, to espouse the Princess Jane, or do anything else his patron wished; and then, ambitious of emulating his predecessors, the third Edward put himself at the head of a powerful army in order to involve the affairs of Scotland once more in blood and confusion, and to place Baliol on the throne.

The capture and reduction of Berwick was the first object of the English king; and on uniting his forces with the malcontents of Baliol, he sat down before the town and closely invested it by land and sea. It was vigorously defended by the governor, Sir William Seton, who repulsed an attempt to take the town by storm, and also contrived to burn a portion of the English fleet. The siege now became a blockade, and the inhabitants were reduced to such distress that they agreed to surrender if not relieved by a Scottish army before a certain day, giving hostages to Edward in the meantime, and among these was young Seton, the governor's son. Sir William Keith, at the head of a body of Scots, succeeded in cutting his way into the town; he was chosen governor by the garrison, and refused to comply with the King of England's second summons to capitulate.

Edward then threatened to put the hostages to death. The Scots could not believe he would be guilty of an act so infamous, and remained firm. Nevertheless, they were all put to death; and Thomas Seton, "a brave and handsome young man, was hanged so near the walls that his father could witness his dying struggles." Horror-struck by this scene, the citizens of Berwick clamoured on Keith to surrender, lest worse should befall them at the hands of one so merciless; and he promised to them and to Edward "that the town and castle of Berwick should be unconditionally given up before the hour of vespers, on the 19th July, unless the Scots in the meanwhile could reinforce the garrison with 200 men-at-arms, or defeat the English in a pitched battle."

To prevent the loss of so important a frontier town, the Scottish army, under the new regent, crossed the Tweed on the 18th July, and encamped at Dunse Park, a few miles north of Berwick. Archibald Douglas, Lord of Galloway, who led them, was the brother of Bruce's comrade, the good Sir James, who had fallen in battle against the Moors in Spain. He was a brave man, but an imprudent leader, and was neglecting the dying advice of King Robert, "that the fate of the kingdom should never, if possible, depend on the doubtful issue of a general engagement."

He found the English army strongly posted on the crest of an eminence called Halidon Hill, situated to the westward of the town, with a great body of Irish in their ranks, under Lord Darcy. Of their strength and particular disposition history fails to inform us, save that the traitor Baliol commanded one of the wings, and that a marshy hollow lay in front of their line. The Regent of Scotland divided his army into four columns.

The first was led by John, Earl of Moray, son of the veteran Randolph; but being young and inexperienced, he had to assist him two well-tried soldiers, John and Simon Fraser, of Oliver

Castle, whose father was killed at the battle of Dupplin. The second was led by the Steward of Scotland, a boy of sixteen, assisted by his uncle, Sir James Stewart, of Rosythe, in Fifeshire. The third was led by the regent himself, having with "him the Earl of Carrick; and the fourth, or reserve, was led by Hugh; Earl of Ross. The numbers of the Scottish army are variously stated by historians. The continuator of Hemingburgh, an author of that age, and Knyghton, who lived shortly after, ascertain their strength with more precision than is generally required by historical facts. The former records the Scottish force to have been, besides earls and other great lords and barons, 55 knights, 1,100 men-at-arms on horseback, and 13,500 of the commons, lightly armed - in all 14,655 men. - but the servants, pages, and camp-followers were more numerous than the actual combatants. At noon on the 19th of July they advanced to decide the fate of Berwick, but their leaders exhibited a deplorable lack of all military skill.

As the English were so posted that they could not be attacked by cavalry, the whole of the Scottish knights and men-at-arms dismounted, committed their horses to their pages, and prepared to fight on foot. While drawing near they were severely galled by the English archers, but managed to reach the intervening morass in very good order; but then the disasters of the day began. Impeded in their advance by the soft and spongy nature of the ground, their ranks became broken, while from the crest of the hill the archers poured on them volley after volley of arrows with certain aim and fatal effect. An ancient writer, quoted by Tytler, says, "These arrows flew as thick as motes in the sunbeam,'. and every instant hundreds were wounded or slain. Yet the four columns cleared the swamp, and with levelled lances, eighteen feet in length, made so furious an uphill charge upon the English, that for a few minutes the ranks of the latter were broken, and defeat seemed at hand till their reserve came on. Then, breathless and disordered by their ascent of the eminence, the ill-fated and ill-led Scots were unable to sustain the ground they had won.

After a brief but terrible struggle, they were borne down the lull towards the swamp. The Earl of Ross, in leading the

Charge of the Scots at Halidon Hill.

reserve to attack the flank of the wing led by Baliol, was killed. Fighting in the van, the regent received a mortal wound, and was taken prisoner, with the Earls of Sutherland and Menteith. The Scots gave way on all hands, and as the pages were the first to fly with the horses, very few of the nobles or men-at-arms escaped in the bloody pursuit that ensued and was continued for some miles, chiefly by the Irish kerns, under Lord Darcy. Four thousand Scots and more lay dead on the field. Among these were the aged Malcolm, Earl of Lennox, one of the earliest adherents of Robert Bruce; Alexander Bruce, Earl of Carrick; John Campbell, Earl of Athole, nephew of the late king; John Graham, Alexander Lindesay, and other great barons; the two Frasers; and John, James, and Alan Stuart. "It may be remarked," says Lord Hailes, "that at Halidon two Stewarts fought under the banner of their chief - Alan of Dreghom, the paternal ancestor of Charles I.; and James of Rosythe, the maternal ancestor of Oliver Cromwell." Rapin, from an old authority, states the Scots killed at 36,907 of all ranks, more than twice the number of men in the field.

The victory was won with very inconsiderable loss. It is related by English historians that on the side of their countrymen there were killed one knight, one esquire, and twelve foot-soldiers. "Nor will this appear incredible," says Lord Hailes, "when we remember that the English ranks remained unbroken, and that their archers, at a secure distance, incessantly annoyed the Scottish infantry." Aware that it had been provided by the treaty of capitulation "that Berwick should be considered as relieved in case 200 men-at-arms forced a passage into the town," the Scottish men-at-arms during the action had made a vigorous effort to achieve this, but were opposed by Edward in person, and repulsed with great loss; and after this disastrous battle, on the 20th of July, the town and castle of Berwick were surrendered according to the agreement.

SLUYS

To unite in his own person the crowns of France and England was now the great aim of Edward's policy. The three sons of Philip IV had died without heirs, and Edward III of England and Philip of Valois were rivals for the vacant throne. Edward's mother was a daughter of Philip IV, and Philip was a nephew of that monarch. The Salic Law, which enacts that no female can inherit the French throne, excluded Edward, so Philip was elected. The King of England, whose conduct to France was as lawless and unjustifiable as to his neighbours the Scots, seized all the wool and tar in his crown and his jewels, quartered on his shield and banners the golden lilies of France, assumed "Dieu et mon Droit" as his motto, and sailed to the Continent for the purpose of asserting in battle what he conceived to be his rights; and the year 1340 witnessed a naval engagement which will bear comparison even with the most glorious achievements of more modern times. "The name of Edward III," says Sir Harris Nicolas, "is more identified with the naval glory of England than that of any other of her sovereigns; for though the sagacious Alfred and the chivalrous Richard commanded fleets and defeated the enemy at sea, Edward gained in his own person two signal victories, fighting on one occasion until his ship actually sunk under him, and was rewarded by his subjects with the proudest title ever conferred on a British monarch - ' King of the Sea.'"

Philip of France was duly apprised, by the preparations that were being made in England and the Low Countries, of the designs of Edward upon his crown and kingdom. He fitted out a great fleet, consisting of 400 vessels, which he stationed in the port of Sluys (then considered one of the finest harbours in the world), with 40,000 fighting men on board. Robert of Avesbury relates that on the Saturday fortnight before the feast of St. John the Baptist, "the king was at Orwell, in Suffolk, where there were forty ships or thereabouts, preparing for his passage into Flanders, where he was going to his wife and children, whom he had left in the city of Ghent," where his chief ally was the famous brewer, Jacques van Ardtfeldt, and that he was about to sail in two days; when the Archbishop of Canterbury sent to warn him of the vast force collected by Philip at Sluys, and urged "His Majesty to provide himself with a better squadron, lest he and those who were with him should perish." But the king replied bravely that "he was resolved to sail at all events." The archbishop thereupon quitted his seat at the council, obtained leave to retire, and resigned the Great Seal. On this the king sent Sir Robert de Morley, his admiral, and Sir John Crabbe, another skilful seaman, over to Sluys, and on their return they agreed with the bishop. The king, in anger, said, "You have arranged this with that prelate, in order to stop my voyage; but I shall go without you; and all who are afraid may stay at home!"

Then the admiral and seaman said that they would stake their heads that if the king persisted "in this resolution, he and all who went with him would certainly be destroyed; yet that they were ready to follow him, even unto certain death." On this Edward sent for the archbishop, and prevailed upon him to resume the care of the Great Seal, and then he issued his orders to all the ports both in the north and south of England, and to the Londoners, to send him aid; so that within ten days he had a navy said to consist of 260 sail, with which he appeared off Sluys on the feast of St. John the Baptist. Other writers say that he had the French fleet reconnoitred by the Lords Reginald de Cobham and John de Chandos, who reported that it was alike powerful and numerous. On this the king put on his armour, and exclaimed, with joy, "For this opportunity I have long wished; and, by the help and blessing of God and St. George, I shall now engage them, and avenge my wrongs! "

This was a very gratuitous oath on Edward's part, as history has failed to record that he had any "wrongs" to complain of - his wars with France being as wanton and as wicked as his wars with Scotland.

Schomberg, in his "Naval Chronology," says that "Edward gave the necessary directions for forming his line and the mode of attack with as much dexterity as if he had been bred to the sea." He certainly displayed that genius for the art of war which always characterised him. He formed his fleet in two lines; the first consisted of his largest and stoutest ships, to bear the brunt of the encounter; each alternate ship being filled by archers, and crossbow-men, with men-at-arms. The second line was a mere reserve, to be drawn upon if necessary.

At eight o'clock in the morning the battle began by the enemy advancing with the *Great Christopher*, a ship taken by them in the preceding year from the English, and the ships throwing their grappling-irons on board each other, till the whole resembled a vast raft; and then ensued a close and murderous hand-to-hand fight with pike and dagger, sword and axe. The French fought with resolute bravery, and a vast number of them were slain or driven overboard into the sea. For eleven hours the fight continued, and at seven in the evening it was likely to be a drawn battle; when it was begun a second time with renewed fury, for the French galleys, on attempting to escape in the twilight, were assailed more resolutely than ever. One large craft, called the *St. Jacques de Dieppe*, with many others, was sunk; for of the whole French fleet, only thirty escaped, all being taken or destroyed; and these, says Knyghton, the king ordered Sir John Crabbe - a Fleming, formerly in the service of the King of Scotland - to pursue with forty sail, but he failed to overtake them in the dark. The prudence, resolution, and bravery of Edward won him the admiration of all, particularly of "the mariners, who were amazed to see him give orders with such foresight that one would have thought he had commanded at sea all his life." He lost 4,000 men, and one great ship, a galley of Hull, was sunk with all hands by a shower of stones, a somewhat singular kind of broadside, but one common enough in those days. The French lost their two admirals and nearly 12,0.00 men, and Edward kept the sea for three days with all his banners flying, to put his victory beyond all dispute; and save his court buffoon, no man in France dared tell Philip the terrible story of the destruction of his armament. Walsingham states that the jester came into his presence in a seeming passion, and exclaimed, "Cowardly Englishmen! Dastardly, faint-hearted Englishmen!" Then Philip asked him why he called them so.

"Because," replied the jester, "they durst not leap out of their ships into the sea, as the brave Frenchmen did." Walsingham tells us that in this battle many guns were taken from the French.

Six years after this we find Edward at the siege of Calais, with a fleet of 738 sail, manned by 15,000 men, "which," says a pleasant writer, "gives an average of about twenty men to a ship about the size of a merchantman's long-boat! So, after all, it was but a fleet of midges - a fleet that the Sandwich Islanders have surpassed in more barbarous days."

De Mezeray alleges discord between the two French admirals to have been the cause of their defeat at Sluys on the 24th of June. Edward's exploits there so raised the ardour of the English Parliament that they were eager for the prosecution of the war, and he speedily found himself at the head of 100,000 Englishmen, at home and abroad (besides 40,000 Flemings), and of these 30,000 sailed from Southampton to win the field of Cressy, and cut their way to the gates of Calais.

CRESSY, 1346

EDWARD LANDED at La Hague, in Normandy, on the 26th August, and his first act was to knight his son - a mere boy, the Prince of Wales - the future Black Prince of glorious memory. His army consisted of 4,000 men-at-arms, 10,000 archers, 12,000 Welsh and 4,000 Irish infantry. He divided it in three divisions, which marched separately in the day, but all formed one camp at night. They ravaged the country with great atrocity, and the towns of Valognes, St Lo, Charenten, and Harfleur were plundered and partially destroyed.

Considerable alterations had now been made in the armour worn; a visored bascinet was used by knights in the field, the crested helmet being reserved for the lists alone. The casing of the body in jointed armour was now nearly complete, and the adoption of breast and back plates enabled soldiers to dispense with the ancient hauberk of rings. The use of plate-armour was a decided improvement, being lighter than the chain with its accompanying garments. The magnificent jupon, emblazoned with the wearer's arms, and the splendid knightly girdle, are both the testimonies of a warlike age; greaves, or jambs (steel boots), and sollerets to cover the feet had been introduced. The backs of the gauntlets were furnished with overlapping plates, armed with knobs or spikes of iron. Those of Edward the Black Prince were of brass; and Camden, but without authority, says that he adopted the famous triple plume, or "Prince of Wales's feathers," by slaving John, King of Bohemia, who wore such a plume, at Cressy, but it is very unlikely that so gallant a prince would have slain with his own hand the aged and blind monarch referred to. He is also said to have worn at Cressy, as afterwards Henry V did at Agincourt, a heart-shaped ruby, which is now in the new crown that was- made for Queen Victoria. By this time cross-bows were in pretty general use among the English. These were of different kinds, such as the latch, the prodd, &c., but they all carried indifferently arrows, darts, quarreaux or bolts of iron, and stone or leaden bullets. The common range of a point-blank shot was from forty to sixty yards, with an elevation of 1:20; Crossbow-men were dressed like other archers, but sometimes fought on horseback. But a new era in war was to be inaugurated, for with the army of Edward III came five pieces of small cannon, a species of weapon supposed to be unknown in France, though cannon are spoken of in a sea engagement in the thirteenth century, between the King of Tunis and a Moorish King of Seville. By whom the five pieces of ordnance were made

Edward III knighting the Black Prince.

is uncertain; but Le Blond, in his "Treatise of Artillery," says that the earliest guns "were of a very clumsy and inconvenient make, being usually formed of several pieces of iron fitted together lengthwise, and then hooped with iron rings; and as they were used for throwing stones of prodigious weight, in imitation of the ancient machines, they were of enormous bore. But the difficulty of conducting and managing these pieces, and the discovery that iron bullets of much less weight might be impelled by better powder, soon introduced the present fabric and matter of cannon."

Edward's Welsh and Irish were light and disorderly troops, more fitted for plunder and pursuit than a steady encounter with the well-armed soldiery of France, and even the best men of his army were but newly levied and unused to war; but they committed fearful ravages, in most instances sparing neither sex nor years. At length Philip advanced against Edward, at the head of 100,000 men; and the latter, afraid of being surrounded in an enemy's country, began a retreat towards Flanders. In this retrograde movement occurred the famous passage of the Somme, at the ford of Blanchetaque, all the bridges being either strongly guarded or broken down. Under Godemar de Faye, 20,000 Frenchmen held the opposite bank; but Edward threw himself into the river sword in hand, at the head of his troops, and forced the passage, and reached in security the opposite bank with his whole force, just as Philip and his vast army reached the river and the tide was rising. Thus on a few moments depended the fate of Edward III; and, by his presence of mind and celerity, these moments were turned from ruin to victory, for the justly infuriated French would have wreaked terrible vengeance on him and his army. He then continued his march, and took up a position at the village of Cressy, or Creci en Ponthieu, on advantageous ground, and there awaited the enemy. In Froissard we find a description of how the English army passed the night before Cressy, one of the most memorable battles of the age.

The king lay in the fields with his host, and made a supper to all his chief lords and knights. "And when they were all departed to take their rest, then the king entered into his oratory and kneeled down before the altar, praying God devoutly that if he fought the next day, he might achieve the journey to His honour. Then, about midnight, he laid him down to rest, and in the morning he rose betimes and heard mass; and his son, the Black Prince, with him, and the most of his company, were confessed and houseled. And after the mass he commanded every man to be armed and to draw to the field, to the place before appointed. Then the king caused a park to be made by the roadside behind his host, and there were set all the carts and carriages, and within the park were all their horses, for every man was afoot; and into this park there was but one entry."

As far as we can calculate, it was now the morning of Saturday, the 6th of August, 1346, though some writers give a different date. The English army was formed in three divisions on the grassy slope, and all lay on the ground till they saw the French army moving across the plain towards them, rending the air with shouts, such as, "Down with them!" "Let us slay them!" Then the archers assumed their bows and salades (or helmets), and every man stood in his ranks. A great flock of ravens were seen to hover' over the French army, and this, says De Mezeray, "was deemed a presage of their defeat." But there was a natural cause for their appearance, as the morning of the battle broke with storm and rain, thunder and lightning - "a fitting prelude for a day of blood."

The first line of the English was commanded by Edward the Black Prince, so called from the colour of his armour, and, as a French historian adds, , also from his sable plumes. Under him were the Earls of Warwick, Oxford, and Harcourt; the Lords

Chandos and Holland, and other nobles. The second line was led by the Earls of Arundel and Northampton, with the Lords Basset, Willoughby, and Roos, and Sir Lewis Tufton. The king in person led the third line, with which he proposed to support, if needful, the two first, or secure a retreat for the whole in case of defeat. He formed trenches to protect his flanks and secure his baggage in the wood. With the English army were 6,000 Irish.

Philip had also divided his army into three great columns. The first consisted of 15,000 Genoese crossbow-men, led by Antonio Doria and Carlo Grimaldi. The second was led by the Count d'Alençon, brother to the king, who had on this occasion no less than three other crowned heads serving under his banner - John of Luxembourg, the aged King of Bohemia, who had lost one eye in battle" against the pagans of Lithuania, and been rendered totally blind of the other by a Jewish quack; the King of the Romans, his son; and the King of Majorca, who had been driven from the Balearic Isles three years before, by Pedro IV, of Arragon. United with the force of Godemar de Faye, the French army now mustered 120,000 men all told, in their helmets. Hume asserts that Philip had cannon, but in his haste left them behind, a very unlikely circumstance if he possessed them at all. The "*Dictionnaire Militaire*" (1758) asserts that cannon "were known in France," according to some authors, in 1338, under Philip, but known of only. "Nevertheless," says Voltaire, "till the reign of Charles VIII artillery continued in its infancy; such is the force of inveterate customs, and so slow the progress of human industry. They did not make use of artillery in sieges till the reign of Charles V, King of France; and the spear was their principal weapon till the reign of Henry IV."

The French, in their enthusiasm, had marched in great haste; and the heavily-accoutred Genoese, weary after a march of six leagues, carrying their cross-bows, were already beginning to fail: and when Philip said, "Make the Genoese go on in front, and begin the battle, in the name of God and St. Denis!" they muttered, and, in the words of Froissard, said to their constables, "We be not well ordered to fight this day; we be not in the case to do any great deed of arms, and have more need of rest." Then said the Count d'Alençon, commander of the second line, with scorn, "Truly, a man is well at ease to be charged with these kind of rascals, who are faint and fail us now when most at need!"

Now the sun came forth brilliantly in rear of the English, but shone full into the eyes of the. French. The Genoese continued to advance, whooping, yelling, and making many antics; "but the English stood still and stirred not." This whooping the Genoese continued, adds Froissard, whose description we chiefly follow, till they came within range; but the recent rains had relaxed the strings of their arblasts, so that the bolts fell short. The English archers drew their bows from their cases dry and serviceable - those splendid six-foot bows, on which the glory of England so often depended.

"Then," says the knightly historian, "the English archers each stepped forth one pace (as he drew the bowstring to the ear), and let their arrows fly so wholly and so thick that it seemed as snow." The cloth-yard shafts soon quivered in the faces, breasts, and arms of the Genoese, who fell into) immediate disorder; some cut the strings of their cross-bows, others cast them away, and the whole began to recoil upon the heavily-mailed men-at-arms of the Count d'Alençon.

"Slay those rascals," cried Philip of France; "they do but hinder and trouble us without reason." Then their own cavalry dashed among them, and killed a great many, while the English arrows fell fast among both; and, to add to the general confusion, the cannon - now heard in battle for the first time - belched forth a storm of stones upon the wild mêlée. Then nothing was seen in that vast body but hurry and confusion, terror and dismay. The Welsh and Irish now began to creep forward, with great knives or daggers, and slew, by stabs and gashes in the throats, great numbers of the dismounted French knights and men-at-arms, who were simply wounded, or rolling helplessly amid the press in their heavy armour. Then it was that the old blind King of Bohemia, when the state of affairs was explained to him, said to those about him, "Sire, ye are my men, my friends, and companions; I require you to lead me so far forward that I may strike one stroke with my sword."

Then two knights buckled the reins of their bridles to those of his horse, lest they should lose him in the press, and the three charged together. / The aged king "struck a stroke with his sword, yea, and more than four, and fought valiantly, and so did all his company; but they adventured so fat-forward that they were all slain, and the next day were found in the place about the king, with their horses tied to each other."

This was about three in the afternoon.

The young Prince of Wales had presence of mind to take advantage of the confusion, and led his line to the charge. The French cavalry had by this time freed themselves of the Genoese runaways, and, by superior numbers and steady hand-

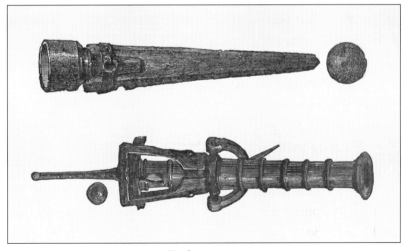

Early cannon.

to-hand fighting, began to hem young Edward round. The Earls of Northampton and Arundel now advanced to his aid; and soon the battle became hot and terrible. From the summit of the hill of Cressy, the king, near a windmill, was looking on, when a messenger from Warwick came, clamouring for succour. Then said the king, "Is my son dead, or hurt, or on the earth felled?" No, sire," replied the knight; "but he is overmatched, and hath need of your aid." "Return to my son," said Edward, "and tell him that to him I reserve the honour of the day. I am confident he will show himself worthy of the honour of that knighthood which I so lately conferred upon him; and that, without my assistance, he will be able to repel the enemy."

This message added to the ardour of Warwick and the prince. A fresh charge with redoubled vigour was made upon the French, by which the whole line of cavalry was thrown into disorder, and the Count d'Alençon was killed; and then flight followed the confusion. Philip of France remained on the field till the last, when the evening was closing in, unwilling to believe that all was lost. When no more than threescore knights remained about him, one, named Sir John of Heynault, who had remounted him after his horse had been killed by an arrow, said, "Sire, depart while there is yet time; lose not yourself wilfully. If this field is lost, you shall recover it again another season." They galloped away, and now the flight became general. The Welsh infantry rushed into the throng, and, with their long knives, cut the throats of all who had fallen; nor was any quarter given that day by the victors."

Philip rode to the castle of La Broyes, where he found the gates closed, for the night was dark; but the captain came to the walls, and asked, "Who calleth there at this time of night?"

"Open your gate quickly," cried Philip, "for this is the fortune of France."

The sorrowful captain recognised the king; he let down the

bridge and opened the gate: and when Philip entered he had with him but Sir John of Heynault and five other barons.

On his return to camp the Black Prince, who had distinguished himself in a manner so remarkable, was embraced by the king his father.

"My brave son!" he exclaimed, "persevere in your honourable course. You are indeed my son, for valiantly have you acquitted yourself this day, and shown yourself worthy of empire."

The young prince then went on his knees and craved his father's blessing, and the night was spent in feasting and rejoicing. The recorded results of this battle would seem exaggeration, were they not so well authenticated. Won as it was chiefly by the bow, the English loss was so small that it has never been stated; but that of the French was terrible. Besides the Kings of Bohemia and Majorca and the Count d'Alen on, there fell the Duke of Lorraine; Lewis de Creci, Count of Flanders; and eight other counts two archbishops, the Count de Blois, 1,200 knights, and 30,000 soldiers. Such was the cost to humanity of one day's proceedings, in the unjust endeavour to conquer France.

Eighty standards were taken. Among these was the beautiful banner of the King of Bohemia, embroidered in gold, charged with three ostrich feathers, and the German motto "*Ich Dien*" which, says Rapin (after Camden probably), was brought to the Prince of Wales, who assumed therefrom his well-known crest and motto. But this favourite tradition is unsupported by history; for on the seal appended to a grant of the prince's to his brother, John of Gaunt, dated 1370, twenty-four years after Cressy, he appears with a *single* feather, while the crest of John of Bohemia in that battle was a single eagle's pinion. The triple plume, now known as that of the Prince of Wales, was first adopted by Henry Stuart, the young and gallant son of James I of England and VI of Scotland, who, like the Black Prince, died before his father.

On the day subsequent to the battle, by displaying the captured French standards, many of the country people, who were ignorant of the general result, were lured towards the English camp, where a pitiful slaughter was made of them by 500 lances and 2,000 archers, dispatched for that special purpose. Edward remained for three days to bury the dead, some of whom he interred at Montreuil; and then he marched through the Boulonnois to lay siege to Calais, that he might always have an open gate into France. It may be interesting to give here a statement of the pay of the English troops in Normandy and before Calais at this time, as given in the Appendix to "Brady's History of England" (Vol. II, p. 88). They consisted of 31,294 combatants, whose subsistence for 131 days amounted to £127,201 2s. 9d.

"To Edward Prince of Wales, being in the king's service, in Normandy, France, and before Calais, with his retinue, for his wages of war, 4s. a day; 102 knights, each 2s. a day; 264 esquires, each i2d. a day; 384 archers on horseback, each 6d. a day; 69 foot archers, each 3d. a day; 513 Welshmen, whereof one chaplain, at 6d. a day, one physician, one herald, 5 ensigns, 25 sergeants or officers over twenty men, each 4d. a day, 480 footmen, each 2d. a day.

"To Henry of Lancaster, being in the king's service before Calais, with his retinue and one other earl, each 6s. 8d. a day; eleven bannerets, each 4s. a day; 193 knights, each 2s. a day; 512 esquires, each 12d. a day; 46 men-at-arms and 612 archers on horseback, each 6d. a day.

"To William de Bohun, Earl of Northampton (K.G. in T350), and his retinue, at the same rate.

"To Thomas Hatfield, Bishop of Durham, 6s. 8d. per day; 3 bannerets, 48 knights, 164 esquires, 81 archers on horseback, as above."

Knights-bannerets were generally created on the field, and

the form of creation was simply performed by the candidate presenting his pennon to the king or general, who cut off the train and made it square; hence they were sometimes known as knights of the square banner, marking authority over a troop capable of forming a solid square of from ten to fifteen men per face. Hence the term "squadron."

While Edward was pressing with famine and steel the siege of Calais, where John de Vienne held him at bay for nearly a year, there occurred an event at home, and only two months subsequent to the splendid victory at Cressy, which, like it, did singular honour to the English arms.

DURHAM, 1346 -
WINCHELSEA, 1349

DURHAM

INDUCED BY the urgent entreaties of the King of France, now sorely pressed by the invading army of England, David II, King of Scotland, was lured into war with that country. He accordingly assembled a numerous army at Perth, where a body of troops from the Highlands and Islands of Scotland appeared at the royal muster-place; but a deadly feud which existed between Ronald, Lord of the Isles, and the Earl of Ross, led to the assassination of the former in the monastery of Elcho, at the instigation of the latter, who, dreading the king's vengeance, retired with all his followers, and sought refuge in the mountains. Then the men of the Isles, enraged by the unpunished murder of their chief, returned home in confusion; and by this, feud the king's host was sensibly diminished in number, yet he commenced his march for England at the head of 50,000 men. Though possessing but little of his father's judgment, and less of his military skill, David had all the hereditary valour of his house, and made the utmost haste on his expedition.

He entered England by the western frontier, with a force stated variously by Froissard at 50,000, by Speed at 62,000, and by Knyghton at 36,000, and more probably with truth, 2,000 of these were cavalry in complete armour; and though the Scots used cannon so early as 1340, there is no record of their having as yet such engines in the field. He stormed the Moat of Liddel, which was defended by Walter Selby, a celebrated freebooter, whom he beheaded. He was one of the band of robbers, so famous in English story, who pillaged two cardinals and the

Bishop of Durham, when they came towards Scotland to publish the Pope's most unjust sentence of excommunication against the Scottish people for resisting England, on the plea that by doing so they retarded the progress of the Holy War! The garrison of the Moat were put to the sword. At this early stage of the expedition, Douglas, the Knight of Liddesdale, recommended its abandonment, to the indignation of the other Scottish barons.

"What!" they exclaimed; "must we fight for your gain? You have profited by the spoils of England, and do you grudge us our share? Never had we such an opportunity for taking just vengeance on our enemies. Edward and his chief commanders are absent, and here are none to oppose our progress save churchmen and base artisans."

In this reply to Sir William Douglas, the barons particularly alluded to the storming of the Moat of Liddel, which was connected with the western territories of Liddesdale, and served as a frontier garrison against his castle of Hermitage. Then the king continued his march, and, crossing the Tyne at a place called Ryton, above the town of Newcastle, advanced into the Bishopric of Durham, where, according to the legendaries, St. Cuthbert appeared to him in a vision one night, and besought him to save the property of the Church from pillage and sacrilege. On the 16th of October, 1346, at nine in the morning, he halted and encamped at Beaurepair, or Bear Park, in the parish of St. Oswalds, at Durham, a beautiful ecclesiastical retreat, which had been defaced and ruined by the Scots in the time of Edward II; but its remains still exist, pleasantly situated on an eminence two miles from the city, having a long, extended, level meadow to the south.

Meanwhile, unknown to King David, Henry de Piercy, Ralph de Neville, Musgrove, Scrope, Hastings, and other great northern barons, were assembling forces to repel him. With them was the ubiquitous Edward Baliol - for in those days the

Baliols were to Scotland what the Bonapartes are to France - and they were further reinforced by the Church vassals of the Archbishops of Canterbury and York, by those of the Bishops of Durham, Carlisle, and Lincoln, and by 10,000 trained soldiers, who had been about to depart for the closer siege of Calais. Their muster-place was the park of Bishop Auckland; and their whole strength is said to have been 1,200 men-at-arms, 3,000 archers, and 17,000 infantry.' Many monks were in the ranks, a proof of useless zeal, when so many of the northern lords and sheriffs were present in arms. Froissard has asserted that Queen Philippa was their leader, and other historians of both countries have followed him implicitly. "A comely princess, the mother of heroes, at the head of an army in absence of her lord, is an ornament to history," says Lord Hailes; "yet no English writer of considerable antiquity mentions this circumstance, which, if true, they would not have omitted."

On the morning of the 17th October they were only six miles distant from the Scots, to oppose whose progress they marched

Beaurepair Abbey.

towards Sunderland Bridge, intending, doubtless, to barricade and defend it by archers. The Knight of Liddesdale who had advanced on a foraging expedition at the head of the men-at-arms alone, suddenly came upon the entire English army on the march, near the Ferry-of-the-Hill. He endeavoured to elude an encounter, but was compelled to fight, and had his brother taken prisoner and 500 of his best men slain; while he escaped with difficulty, to alarm the Scottish camp, where all were now under arms and prepared for battle.

David formed his army in three' divisions. The" first was led by the High Steward of Scotland and the Earl of March; the second by the Earl of Moray and Sir William Douglas of Liddesdale, then named "The Flower of Chivalry;" the third, which consisted of select troops, the principal knights, many nobles, and a party of French auxiliaries, was led by the king in person.

Advancing by the Red Hills, on the west of the city of Durham, the English were gradually drawing near the ground on which the battle was to be fought. It was hilly, and in some places so steep towards the river Wear that it is singular how masses of men could manoeuvre in such a place. Notwithstanding the repulse of Douglas, King David considered the English a raw and undisciplined army, and evinced the utmost eagerness to begin the encounter. He felt certain of victory, •as his soldiers did of the spoil of Durham. In front of the English army, amid the banners of the nobles, was borne a great crucifix; and the monks of Durham, aware that they might be pillaged without ceremony if the Scots were victorious, had resort to that which in those days was easily believed in - a miracle. On the night before the battle, it was said, the Prior of Durham, John Fossour, had a holy vision, in which he was commanded to take the sacred corporal cloth with which St. Cuthbert was wont to cover the chalice when he had celebrated mass, to place it on a spear, and next morning to repair to the Red Hills, where he was to remain with it until the close of the battle. The English advanced in four divisions. Lord Henry Piercy led the first, supported by the Bishop of Durham, and several nobles of the northern counties; the second was led by William de la Zouche, the Archbishop of York, accompanied by the Bishop of Carlisle, and the Lords Neville and Hastings; the third was led by the Bishop of Lincoln, the Lord Mowbray, and Sir Thomas Rokeby; the fourth was led by the Archbishop of Canterbury, Lord de Roos, and the Sheriff of Northumberland. With this division rode Edward Baliol, who some writers assert commanded it. Each of these divisions consisted of above 4,000 men, and each had an accompaniment of horse and archers. Fordun, and some others, enumerate the latter at 20,000. Be that as it may, Sir John Grahame, who was now Earl of Menteith, remembering how a quick cavalry movement against the archers had decided the field of Bannockburn, asked leave to attack them. "Give me but one hundred horse," said he, "and I shall undertake to disperse them all." But David declined. Meanwhile, as the adverse lines were drawing nearer, with all their arms and armour glittering in the sunshine, the monks of Durham, in obedience to the prior's, vision, were busy on a hillock called the Maiden's Bower. There they were offering up their prayers for the success of their countrymen, on their knees around the holy relic of St. Cuthbert. This banner-cloth has been, described as being a yard broad and five quarters deep, "the bottom indented in five parts, all fringed and made fast about with red silk and gold.

It was made of red velvet, on both sides embroidered with flowers of green silk and gold; and in the midst was the corporal cloth enclosed, covered over with white velvet, half a yard square every way, having a cross of red velvet on both sides; and then five little silver bells fastened to the said banner-cloth, like unto sacring-bells." During the whole time of the conflict the monks also occupied themselves in forming and erecting "a beautiful wooden cross, in remembrance of the holy banner being borne to the battle."

The first blow was struck by Sir John Grahame, who attacked the archers, in his anxiety to scatter them, at the head of his own private followers; but these being far too few in numbers to make any impression, were speedily beaten off, and their brave leader had a narrow escape, as his horse was shot under him.

At nine in the morning the Scots commenced a general attack, by order of the king. The High Steward led the vanguard, the advance of which was sorely impeded by walls and hedges, from behind which they were galled by the. English archers, whose arrows flew thick as hail; while the men-at-arms and bill-men, pouring through the gaps made in the ranks by those field enclosures, charged the Scots in a confused but desperate manner. Nevertheless, the latter came on with such impetuous fury that, by sheer dint of sword and battle-axe, they hurled the first English column back in confusion against that of Lord Piercy. At this crisis the renegade Baliol is said to have rushed into the thickest of the mêlée with a body of horse, the weight of which threw the Scots into confusion, and gave the first column of the English time to reform. Here the Earl of Moray fell, and the Knight of Liddesdale was taken prisoner; while the High Steward was compelled to retreat and reorganise his troops, who were entangled among hedges and ditches, where they had little room to act. Baliol was too wary to follow in that direction, but flung himself, with all who would obey him, on the flank of that division which was led by the King of Scotland, around whom all the tide of battle rolled. In spite of every disadvantage, the conflict was maintained for three hours; and amid the most furious charges from the English men-at-arms, and the slaughter made by the unerring shafts of their archers, the king, surrounded by his nobles and knights, fought valiantly. The Scots had now completely given way, yet the 'son of the great Bruce repeatedly brought masses of them back by his exhortations and example"; but by twelve o'clock the royal banner was beaten down, and on seeing it fall, the whole division of the Great Steward and of the Earl of March, despairing alike of being able either to rescue the king or retrieve the fortune of the field, quitted it and retreated *en masse*, a circumstance which it is said that David ever remembered and never forgave; yet that the Steward did not retire without severe loss is evident from the great number of barons and gentlemen of the name of Stewart who fell on that day.

When only eighty Scottish gentlemen remained about him, at last the king was taken. Proud, fiery, active, and strong, in the prime of life, and not yet in his fortieth year, David, "though he had two spears hanging in his body, his leg almost incurably wounded, and his sword beaten out of his hand, disdaining captivity, provoked the English by opprobrious language to kill him; and when Sir John Copeland, of Northumberland, advised him to yield, he struck the knight on the face with his gauntlet so fiercely that he knocked out two of his teeth. But, however, Copeland conveyed him out of the field a prisoner. Upon his refusing to deliver him up to the queen, who stayed at Newcastle during the battle, the king sent for him to Calais, where he excused his refusal so handsomely that he sent him back with a reward of five hundred pounds a year in land, where he himself should choose it, near his own dwelling, and made him a knight-banneret." The armour which David wore on that day is said to be still preserved at Raby Castle.

As usual in detailing these Scottish and English battles, the loss of the latter is not mentioned, though one writer states that only four knights and five esquires fell, and that Lord Hastings was mortally wounded; but we may safely conclude that in such a battle, and one so bitterly contested, many Englishmen must have fallen, and not a few of high rank among them.

Of the Scots the slaughter was undoubtedly great, for there fell the Earls of Moray (Randolph, last of his line), Maurice of Strathearn, Hay of Errol (the High Constable), Charteris (the High Chancellor), Peebles (the Lord Chamberlain), more than thirty other nobles, and about 15,000 soldiers, as recorded by Fordun and Knighton. With the king were taken prisoners the Earls of Fife, Menteith, Sutherland, and Wigton, and fifty other barons and knights. In addition to the wounds enumerated, David had also received two from arrows. Knighton mentions one in the head, and Fordun speaks of another as being so deep that the barb could not be extracted, till it came forth when he was praying at the shrine of St Modan, in Fifeshire.

Escorted by 20,000 men, the King of Scotland was conveyed in triumph to London, where he was shown to the citizens on a tall black horse; and in the procession which conveyed him through the streets, the civic authorities and all the guilds or companies of the city took part, clothed in their appropriate costumes. Until he could ransom himself, the royal captive and his companions in misfortune were secured in the Tower, where, by a mean and ungenerous parsimony, unworthy of his position, Edward III compelled them to maintain themselves. He did worse; for on the miserable plea that the Earl of Menteith was a traitor to Baliol, he had him executed with all the shocking barbarities then sanctioned by the English law of treason.

Tradition asserts that many jewels and banners found on the field, together with the famous Black Cross or Rood of Scotland, which was in the hands of St. Margaret when she died in the castle of Edinburgh, were offered to the shrine of St. Cuthbert at Durham, where thanks were offered up for the victory.

"No man could ever know of what wood or metal the cross was made - it was of pure and massive gold on the pedestal, which was garnished all about with rich and large diamonds, precious rubies, turquoises, and emeralds, and placed on a pillar near St. Cuthbert, in the south aisle of the cathedral" (*"Scotia Rediviva"*). David's ransom was finally fixed at 90,000 merks sterling, to be paid at the rate of 10,000 merks annually for nine years; and during those years there was to be a truce between the two kingdoms.

Such was the battle of Durham, or Neville's Cross, as it is frequently called, from a beautiful stone cross erected by Lord Neville on the field, to commemorate the English victory. There were seven steps round the pedestal, which measured four feet nine inches square. The Neville arms, a saltire, &c., were carved thereon, also the effigies of "our Saviour Christ crucified, the picture of the Blessed Virgin on one side, and of St. "John the Evangelist on the other." It remained till the year 1589, when, according to a writer quoted by Ridpath, in his "Border History," "the same was broken down and defaced by some lewd and wicked persons."

Had Edward Baliol fallen in battle at Durham, the bravery of such an end might have atoned for the political errors of his past life. His claims to royalty he forfeited by treason to Scotland. He spent the remainder of his days in obscurity, and died childless, in 1363.

WINCHELSEA

Some fighting on the seas followed shortly after the English victories at Cressy and Durham, and this time with a different nation, with whom, in fact, England had been for some time at peace, but with whom she was destined in years to come to have many a bitter struggle for the dominion of the sea.

It would seem that in 1349 the Spaniards conceived it necessary to exact from England revenge for certain piracies alleged to have been perpetrated by her warlike skippers on the high seas. They sent a squadron up the Garonne, where they found several English vessels, a little leaky, but all deeply laden with wine. Though the King of England was then at peace with the princes of Castile and Arragon, the Spaniards boarded the vessels, murdered the crews, made capture of everything, and then I bore away. Edward III was not a monarch who would submit tamely to an outrage such as this. Fitting out a fleet of fifty sail, he put the Black Prince on board with a body of troops, and embarking himself, sailed from Sandwich in quest of these corsairs, who were now forming portion of a richly-laden Spanish fleet of merchantmen on their homeward way from Flanders. On the 29th of August, 1349, he came up with them, in sight of Winchelsea, off the coast of Sussex, and then Lancaster, Salisbury, Warwick, Arundel, Gloucester, and all the great lords who were with him, prepared for battle and it is alleged that in this sea-fight cannon were first used on board ship by the English, but there is not any very precise or reliable information on the point.

The Spanish fleet numbered forty-four great vessels, described as carracks. King Edward bore resolutely down upon them, grappled with chains and hooks, and engaged. "The Spaniards, defending themselves with obstinate bravery, and preferring death to bondage, rejected with disdain the quarter that was offered them."

The king defeated them, took twenty of their vessels, and sunk others with all on board; but a few set all sail and escaped in the dark. The prizes were laden with woollen cloths and valuable stuffs, the produce of the looms of the industrious Flemings; and to commemorate this battle, Edward had a gold coin struck, whereon he is represented in the middle of a single-masted ship, with his sword, crown, and shield - the latter charged"with the arms of France and England quarterly; the arms of pretence being in the first and fourth cantons of the shield.

This battle off Winchelsea is chiefly remarkable for the alleged adoption of cannon at sea, and, moreover, the mariner's compass was now in use. All the weapons used on land were then used at sea; and in addition to these was the falcastrum, a sort of bill or guisarma, described as a scythe attached firmly to a very long spear. The shape was afterwards preserved, in the double-bladed weapon formed of one piece of iron, and called the guisarma, down to the close of the fifteenth century. Then and for long after the balls shot from cannon were of hewn stone. Sometimes the Scots used gun-stanes, or large pebbles lapped in sheet, lead.

POICTIERS, 1356

PHILIP OF France was dead, and John I, his son, was on the throne. Edward of England had now, awakened thoroughly from the dream of his grasping ambition. Convinced by stern experience that the crown of France lay beyond his reach, he offered to renounce his pretensions thereto by exchanging for them the authority he held as Philip's vassal and liegeman over certain provinces. By Philip this offer had been rejected with contempt, but now his son and successor feigned a willingness to accept of it; but the pride of France was roused. Edward again had recourse to arms, and a plan of combined operations was concerted between him and his son, the Black Prince, who, some historians say, was styled so less from the colour of his plume and armour, than from the circumstance of the French calling him *Le Noir*, on account of the gloom his warlike deeds threw over their country. With some of his companions after-named, he was one of the first Knights of the Garter when the order was founded, six years before.

Advancing from Calais at the head of 60,000 men, the campaign was opened in 1355; and in seven weeks he had laid in ashes five hundred cities, towns, and villages, chiefly in the fertile province of Bordeaux, accompanied by the most shocking barbarities. The harvest was trodden under foot, the people and the cattle were slaughtered together, and all that the army could not consume was wantonly destroyed. The second year's campaign was signalised by the battle of Poictiers. The adventurous prince had pierced too far into the heart of France, and King John, justly provoked by so wanton an invasion, collected an army, also of 60,000 combatants, and made hasty marches to intercept him while occupied before the castle of Remorantin; and the 19th of September saw them engage among the vineyards of Maupertois, near Poictiers, which is the chief city in the department of Vienne.

The army of the prince was now reduced to little more than 14,000 men. It was on the evening of the 17th that the English vanguard fell suddenly on the French rear, and then the prince became aware for the first time that he was outnumbered by 46,000 men, that they swarmed over all the neighbourhood, and that his retreat was cut off.

"God help us!" he exclaimed; "we must consider only how we can best fight them."

He instantly chose an admirable position, on elevated ground, having his flanks protected by vineyard walls and trenches, and to which there was but one approach, a long deep lane between hedgerows, so narrow that only four horsemen could ride through it abreast. In rear of these hedges he placed strong bodies of archers, to gall the enemy as they advanced. Over-night he placed in ambush 300 men-at-arms and 300 archers, at a post from whence they were to make a sudden and unforeseen attack upon the French flank. These men were under Piers, the Captal de Buche, K.G. The English van was commanded by the Earl of Warwick; the rear, or reserve, by the Earls of Salisbury and Suffolk; the main body by the Black Prince himself; while the Lords Sir John de Chandos, K.G., and Audeley, K.G., with other brave and experienced soldiers, were at the head of different corps of the army.

Before a blow was struck, or an arrow shot, the Papal Legate, the Cardinal Tallyrand de Perigord, anxious to prevent the effusion of human blood, offered his services as mediator. He induced the Prince of Wales to promise that he would repair the damages done by his troops; that for seven years he would not bear arms against King John: but the latter scornfully rejected these offers, and, confident in the overwhelming strength of his forces, he would be satisfied with nothing but the surrender of the prince and his whole army at discretion, and, according to Froissard, having four of the leading English nobles "at his mercy."

"I will rather die sword in hand," replied the gallant prince, "than be guilty of deeds so contrary to honour and the glory of the English name!" Then, says Walsingham, he made a short speech to his troops, telling them "that victory depended not. upon numbers, but on bravery; that, for his own part, he was resolved to conquer or die, and would not expose his country to the disgrace of paying his ransom."

This was on Sunday, the 18th, and the day was spent in making fresh trenches, and barricades of wagons, stones, and earth. With earliest dawn on the morning of the 19th, the English trumpets were heard pealing all over Maupertois, calling every man to his feet; and the archers began to bend their bows. Once more the cardinal failed to move the proud resolutions of the King of France.

"Then," said the prince, "let him come on; and God defend the right!" And, doubtless, in that hour of danger, every English heart was animated by the recent memories of Cressy, where they fought with an equal disparity of numbers, and resolved to emulate the courage of those who were the victors there.

John marshalled his host in three divisions, each of 20,000 men. The first was commanded by the Duke of Orleans; with him were a body of German cavalry, and a great band of Scots, who, says Lord Hailes, enjoying a momentary tranquillity at home, crowded to the French standard under Lord William Douglas, who was received with distinguished honours. The second division was led by the dauphin; the third by the king himself, who had by his side Philip, his fourth and favourite son, then only fourteen years of age. So confident were the French of victory, that on this day all the knights wore their richest armour, their most valuable ornaments and orders.

The battle began by a select body of French gendarmerie, led by two marshals; these rode furiously along the lane, but ere they could form in any order to charge or break the front of the English infantry, the archers suddenly opened their deadly volleys from behind the hedgerows. In a few minutes one marshal was shot down, the other was taken prisoner, and the lane become choked with dead or wounded men and horses - the dying rolling over each other in heaps - while, as De Mezeray has it, "the Englishmen's bearded arrows made the horses mad," and in masses they recoiled in terror upon the advancing Germans. This circumstance so alarmed the second column, under the dauphin, that it began to waver in its advance, and many men were seen quietly retreating to the rear. This did not escape the eagle eye of the Black Prince, who at that most critical moment, brought into action the 600 horse and archers

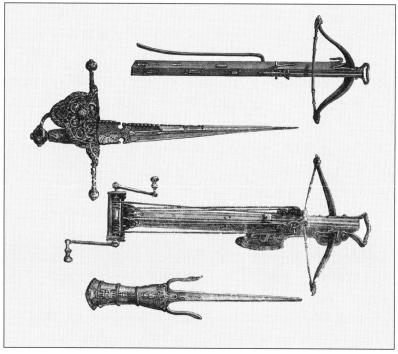

Crossbows and daggers (fourteenth century).

whom he had placed in ambush under the Captal de Buche. The archers shot their volley, and the horse fell on with sword and mace, throwing into confusion by their unexpected attack, the whole left flank of the dauphin's line. A sudden alarm seized the Lords Landas, Bodenai, and St. Venant, to whose care that young prince and two of his brothers had been committed. Anxious for the safety of their charge, they carried them out of the field, most unwisely with a formidable escort of 800 lances, which set an example of flight that was followed almost instantly by the whole division; for since Cressy the French had cherished a wholesome dread of "the green jackets and white bows "of the English archers.

The leading division, under the Duke of Orleans, became seized with a similar panic; and imagining at this early stage of the battle that all was lost, thought no longer of fighting, but began a retreat that speedily became a flight; while the exulting English men-at-arms began to shout, "St. George for Guienne!"

Then said Sir John de Chandos, one of the most able and brilliant warriors of the age, and who had never quitted young Edward's side, "Sire, ride forward; the day is yours! Let us assail the King of France, for with him lies all the strength of the enterprise. Well I know his valour will not permit him to flee; therefore, please God and St. George, he shall remain with us!" Seeing, also that the auspicious moment had arrived, the prince called to the standard - bearers, saying, "Advance, banners, in the name of God and St. George!"

Led by the prince and Chandos, the English men-at-arms poured at full speed through the corpse-encumbered lane, and forming upon a piece of open moor, charged the French with terrible force. Their shock was alike fierce and irresistible-The Constable of France, with many squadrons of horse, vainly endeavoured to hold his ground, but was slain with the chief of his knights; the German horse, under the Counts of Sallebruche,

Nydo, and Nostro, were next cut to pieces; and a terrible carnage was made of the Scots. Lord Douglas was wounded and escaped; but his half-brother, Sir Archibald, was taken prisoner, together with Sir William Baird, of Evandale. The division under the king, inspired by his fine example, fought bravely. He and his principal knights were now on foot, while their assailants were mounted; yet, despite this disadvantage, they made a gallant resistance. Battle-axe in hand, King John fought foremost in the fray; the boy, Philip, by his side, calling to him ever and anon, "Father, guard yourself on the right - guard yourself on the left!"

Around them were the great lords of what was then a noble nation and faithful to its kings, all resolute to die in their defence, though there was death in front and flight in the rear. The prince and Sir John Chandos kept their troops steadily in hand, and concentrated all their efforts on this confused multitude who fought around the king, and who, under axe, arrow, and lance, were falling fast in blood and death. A furious throng of mingled English and Gascons now pressed close upon him, with cries of "Surrender!" He was wounded and beaten to the ground; but again he rose, axe in hand, and continued the unequal combat with furious courage. Anxious to save him, many English gentlemen prayed (among others, Sir John Treffry, a knight of Cornwall) that he would yield; but, being unwilling to do so to any one of inferior rank, the hapless monarch repeatedly asked, "Where is my cousin? Where is the Prince of Wales? "

Then said a young knight of St. Omer, in French, "Sire, surrender; he is not here, but I shall lead you to him."

Struck by the pure accent, the king asked, "Who are you?"

"Sire," replied the other, "I am Denis of Morbeque, a knight of Artois; but I serve the King of England because I have lost my all in France."

"To you I surrender," said John, and presented him with his right-hand gauntlet. As he led him and his son away, the

136

English claimed him with violence from Morbeque; then the Gascons demanded the honour of guarding him; and some, more brutal than the rest, proposed that, rather than yield him to others, he should be put to death: but, luckily for the honour of England, the appearance of Thomas Beauchamp, the Earl of Warwick, K.G., and of Sir John de Pelham, ancestor of the Earls of Chichester, overawed all parties; and, approaching the royal captive with every demonstration of respect, they conducted him to the Prince of Wales.

The English army at Poictiers behaved with more consideration and humanity than was usual with victors in those days, otherwise the slaughter would have been terrible. As it was, the French lost on the field about 8,000 men, of whom 800 were men of family. Among these were the Due de Bourbon, the Due d'Athenes, Constable of France, the Marshal de Nesle, and others; while the king, Prince Philip, thirteen counts, one archbishop, seventy barons and baronets, 2,000 splendidly-accoutred men-at-arms, and a vast multitude of inferior soldiers, remained prisoners in the hands of the Black Prince. Burke

Surrender of the King of France at Poictiers.

records, as a curious circumstance, that the representatives of the four esquires of the Lord Audeley at Poictiers were, by a coincidence, the four aides-de-camp of Sir Rowland Hill in the Peninsular War, four hundred and fifty years later. The Black Prince ordered the body of Robert de Duras, nephew of the Cardinal de Perigord, to be borne away on his shield, according to the etiquette for a knight slain in battle.

The escape of the Scottish prisoner, Archibald Douglas, a warrior famous in the annals of his country, from the English at Poictiers is curiously related by Fordun and Hume of Godscroft. Being arrayed in armour of a very sumptuous kind, he was supposed to be a noble of high rank; and, late in the evening, when some English were about to strip him of it, his friend, Sir William Ramsay, of Collulhie, also a prisoner, anxious he should escape, affected to be furious with passion, and said, "You accursed murderer, how comes it that you are decked in your master's armour? Come hither, and pull off my boots!"

Douglas, who instantly divined his object, knelt down and pulled off one of the boots of Ramsay, who struck him with it; on which some Englishmen interposed, and asked Ramsay "how he dared to so misuse a nobleman of rank?"

"He a nobleman!" exclaimed Ramsay; "why, he is a scullion - a base knave, who I fear has killed his master. Go, villain, to the field, and search for the body of my cousin, your master, that I may give him decent burial." He then ransomed him for forty shillings, and said, "Go - get you gone!"

Douglas carried on the deceit. He was permitted in the dark to search for the body of his pretended master, and was soon beyond the reach of his captors. Most of the prisoners were speedily dismissed - the more important on parole of honour to appear at Bordeaux with their ransoms on a given day - and now came the most splendid and generous chivalry of the Black Prince. In spite of his father's pretensions to the throne of

France, which seemed more than ever feasible, "it was no longer in his eyes," says Sismondi, "John of Valois, who styled himself King of France; it was the true king, whom he acknowledged for the chief of his house, and suzerain of the lordships which he held in France. In the evening he gave a supper to his royal and other distinguished prisoners; but not all the entreaty of King John could induce him to sit down himself at the banquet. His constant reply was - and could words ever have been more delicious to the wounded vanity of a brave man in King John's position? - he 'was not yet qualified to sit at the table of so great a prince and so brave a man.' Seeing that the king took little refreshment, he said, on his knees, "Dear sire, please to make simple cheer. Though God has not been willing to consent to-day to your will, you have on this day won the lofty name of prowess, and have surpassed all the best on your side."

So thus gallantly and nobly did the prince close the day of Poictiers, which was long a household word among the English people. He landed his royal prisoner at Plymouth, according to Walsingham; and on the 24th of the ensiling May he made his entry into London, as the King of Scots had done so recently. He rode a stately white courser, magnificently trapped, and by "his side was the Prince of Wales "on a little black nag:" so studious was he to do honour to his prisoner. He was received by Henry Picard (the same Lord Mayor who so magnificently entertained the four kings at one time in his house, England, Scotland, France, and Cyprus), and by all the aldermen in their robes and the citizens in armour; while all the streets were decked with tapestry and garlands. He was less fortunate than his Scottish companion in misfortune, for he failed to raise the sum of three millions of golden crowns, which were required as his ransom, and eventually died a captive at the Savoy Palace, in the Strand, which was in those days a fashionable and airy country suburb of London.

- C H A P T E R   X I -

THE BLACK PRINCE IN SPAIN - NAJERA, 1367

T HE BATTLE of Najera, or Navaretta, as it was sometimes named, near the Ebro, and the Spanish campaign of the Black Prince, are lightly passed over in English history, as the annalists of those days were more intent on recording the wars with the sister kingdom and troubles at home than on looking much abroad; but these events came to pass in consequence of the prince's supporting the cause of Pedro the Cruel - a cause of which he had soon reason to be ashamed and to deplore.

Pedro had succeeded in 1350 to the throne of Castile, and history cannot show another monarch who was equally perfidious, cruel, debauched, and bloody. He began his reign by the murder of his father's mistress, Leonora de Guzman; daily his nobles fell victims to his suspicion and tyranny; he slew one of his brothers and one of his cousins, in a fit of groundless jealousy; and he caused his innocent queen, Blanche de. Bourbon, of the royal blood of France, to be imprisoned and poisoned, that he might indulge unrestrained in an amour with Maria de Padella, who also died mysteriously. At this crisis, Henry, Count of Trastamare, his natural brother, fearing the ruin of all, took up arms against the tyrant, but failing, fled to France, where he found all men's minds inflamed against Pedro, by the assassination of the French princess; and he craved leave of Charles to enlist the Free Companies under his banner, and lead them into Castile against his brother. Charles V was charmed with the project, and employed the famous Bertrand du Guesclin to negotiate with the 'leaders of those Companies, which were composed of a multitude of military adventurers, who had followed the standard of Edward III in his French wars. They had refused to lay down their arms, or relinquish the mode of life by which they could alone earn subsistence; they therefore associated themselves with other wild spirits, to the number of 40,000 men, as Free Companies or Companions, led by gentlemen of England and Gascony. They were dangerous residents in France, so Charles hailed with joy the double chance of getting rid of them, and having vengeance on Don Pedro.

These Free Lances were also called Malandrins; and the Abbé de Choissi says it was extremely dangerous to oppose them, as they observed a species of discipline in their plundering raids. Their principal leaders were the Chevalier de Verte, Hugues de Coureldé, Robert the Scot, Mathieu de Gournar, and others, all of whom had been solemnly dubbed as knights.

Du Guesclin soon completed his levies; received a sum of 100,000 livres from the Pope, and entered Spain against Pedro, who fled from his dominions and took shelter in Guienne, where he implored the aid of the Black Prince, whom Edward III had invested with the sovereignty of the ceded provinces, as Prince of Aquitaine. De Mezeray avers that jealousy of Du Guesclin's warlike fame led the prince to make the cause of the dethroned monarch his own; anyhow, on obtaining consent of the king, he levied an army against the Count of Trastamare, who had been crowned king at Burgos. On hearing that the Black Prince was approaching the frontiers of Castile, great numbers of the Free Companies, especially those led by Sir Robert Knollys and Sir Hugh Calverley, to the number of 12,000 men as computed by Walsingham, withdrew from Burgos and joined his standard; yet Henry was so beloved by his new subjects that he and Du Guesclin had remaining a force of nearly 100,000 men with which to meet the invader.

The latter, who marched through the deep and beautiful Pass of Roncesvalles, amid tempests of wind and snow, was accompanied by his younger brother, John of Gaunt, created Duke of Lancaster, by John de Chandos, and other companions of Cressy and Poictiers. When he had reached Pampeluna, he received the following letter from the new king, Henry II:

"Enrique, by the grace of God, King of Castile and Leon, of Galicia, Murcia, Jaen, Algarbe, Algeziras, and Gibraltar, Lord of Biscay and Molina. - To the right puissant and most honourable lord, Edward, Prince of Wales and Aquitaine, Duke of Cornwall, and Earl of Chester, greeting: Whereas it is given us to understand that you and your troops have passed the Pyrenees, and are marching towards us, having entered into strict alliance with our enemy, and intend to wage war 'against us; we greatly marvel thereat, since to our knowledge we never offended you, or ever had the least intent so to do. Wherefore, then, are you come against us with such mighty force, to deprive us of that small inheritance which Providence hath allotted us? You have, we acknowledge, the good fortune to be successful in arms above any prince now living, and you magnify yourself in your

The Black Prince's march through Roncesvalles.

142

puissance. But since we know for certain that you intend to give us battle, we also hereby give you to understand as certainly, that whenever you advance into Castile, so surely shall you find us in front, ready to defend and hold this our seignory. Dated at San Domingo de la Calzada."

When the Black Prince had read this letter (which we quote from "The History of Pedro the Cruel"), he said, with his usual spirit, "I well perceive this bastard Henry is a valiant knight, and showeth good courage thus to write us." Then he ordered the Castilian herald to be detained, deeming it unwise to send him back for the present.

While on his march to Salvatierra, near the Zadora, in Alava, Sir Thomas Felton, who, with a troop of Free Lances, had taken post at Navaretta, near King Henry's camp, brought word that the latter had moved thence, and was now at San Miguel; on which the prince marched with all speed as far as the city and plain of Vittoria, at the base of the hills of La Puebla. There he conferred the honour of knighthood on Pedro the Cruel and the Lord Holland, a gallant boy of seventeen (son of his princess by her former husband); the same honour was conferred by the King of Majorca, the Duke of Lancaster, and Chandos on no less than 300 English esquires. But the army soon began to suffer from want of food. The land of Alava was barren, and a small loaf cost a florin. Now tidings came that Henry had moved to Najera; so the prince marched to Logrono, in a fertile plain near the Ebro, which he crossed by a bridge, and began the advance into Castile. But before he quitted his camp at Vittoria, his advanced post, situated on a hill, had been surrounded and cut off; and there fell Sir Thomas Felton and his brother, Sir William, the Earl of Angus, Sir Hugh Hastings, Sir Gaylerd Vigors; and 200 other knights and squires. This happened at a place called Ariniz, a league from Vittoria; and the peasantry to this day call the hill *Los Inglesmonde*, or "The Mount of the English."

The prince's army was now about 30,000 strong. On the 2nd of April he departed from Logrono, and encamped in sight of the enemy, who occupied the little town of Najera, in the district of Rioxo.

In their front flowed the little river Nagerillo, and there, too, lay the road by which Pedro and the prince must pass if they would reach Burgos. There Henry II was determined to meet them, and all his army was eager for battle. The night was spent by both hosts in preparations for that strife which was to decide the fate of Castile; and most quaintly are the details of it chronicled by Froissard, who accompanied Edward in part of the campaign.

"After midnight," we are told, "the trumpet sounded in King Henry's host; then every man armed himself. At the second blast they left their quarters, and were formed in three battles" - i.e., columns.

The first, under Sir Bertrand du Guesclin, consisted of 4,000 knights and esquires, armed and attired after the fashion of France. The second was led by Don Tello and Don Sancho de Castilla, the king's natural brothers, and consisted of lightly-armed cavalry, "mounted on jennets, with a body of infantry, in all 15,000 men. The third, led by Henry in person, with the banner of Castile, consisted of 7,000 horse and 60,000 foot, crossbow-men, and slingers. Prior to mounting his battle charger, Henry rode on a mule along the ranks, "right sweetly praying every man that day to employ himself to defend and keep their honour."

The rising sun showed the smaller army of the Black Prince advancing in fine array, with the white banner of St. George flying, "and it was a great beauty to behold the battalions with all their armour shining." The van of the English was led by John, Duke of Lancaster, and De Chandos.

Before the attack was made, Sir John, or Lord Chandos,

as he was sometimes called, brought to the prince his banner rolled round the staff, and said, "Sir, behold, here is my banner: I require you to display it abroad, and give me leave this day to raise it; for, I thank God and you, I have lands and heritage sufficient to maintain it withal," he added, in allusion to the qualification necessary in a knight who desired to raise his banner, which consisted of at least fifty men-at-arms, with their usual number of pikemen and archers. The prince and Pedro the Cruel took the banner in their hands between them, and unfurled it to the wind; it bore a sharp pyle gules, embroidered on silver. After this he bore the banner to his company, and placed it "in the hands of a good English squire, named William Allestry, who bore it that day and acquitted himself right nobly." Then, adds Froissard, every man, English and Gascon, drew up under their own standards, "and it was great joy," to see all the banners, pennons, and the noble suits of armour that were there. When the English lines began to advance, the Black Prince raised his eyes and his gauntleted hands to heaven, and prayed thus: "Very God, Jesu Christ, who hath formed and created me, consent by your benign grace that I may have this day victory over mine enemies; as that which I do is a rightful quarrel to aid this king chased out of his own heritage." Then, laying his right hand on Don Pedro, who rode by him, he said, "Sir King, ye shall know this day if ever ye shall have any part of the realm of Castile or not. Advance, banners, in the name of God and St. George!"

Then went up the shout "St. George for England!" and the Duke of Lancaster's division flung itself headlong on that led by Du Guesclin and the Marshal Arnauld d'Endreghen. At the first brunt there was a great crashing of spears and clashing of iron shields, while the slings of the Castilians - a weapon which they retained from the Roman days - whirled large stones that did great mischief, till the twang of bows was heard, and the archers of England made their usual havoc among them. Henry's left wing being ill supported, was soon driven back by the prince's right, led on by the Counts D'Armagnac and D'Albert; and as the other divisions closed up the contest became fierce and bloody. The stones of the slingers actually "clave and brake many a bascenet and helm;" but the cloth-yard shafts drove Don Sancho quite out of the field with 2,000 spears, making a passage into the heart of the host for the Captal de Buche and the Lord Clysson, with their companies. "Castile!" was the war-cry on one side, "St. George for Guienne!" on the other; and, in spite of their overwhelming numbers, the Spaniard's began to give way. Henry of Trastamare performed prodigies of valour, and, fighting sword in hand in the front and thickest of the carnage, rallied and reformed the shattered columns no less than three times.

"Lords," he cried, "I am your king; ye have made me King of Castile, and have sworn and promised that to die ye would not fail me. For God's sake, keep your promise, and acquit yourselves with honour!" Then, finding them giving way a fourth time, he cried, with something of despair, "Oh, where is the courage of those noble Spaniards who, under my father, Alphonso, vanquished the Moors? Do not disgrace yourselves this day by flight!"

On the other side, Pedro the Cruel was fighting with the fury of rancorous hate among his own subjects; and history puts some very opprobrious epithets in his mouth, while he called ever and anon, "Where is this Bastard of Trastamare, who calls himself King of Castile! Let him face me if he dare!"

Under Bertrand du Guesclin, the French made the bravest resistance, and kept longer together; but at last he was taken prisoner. Henry's army gave way on all sides, and then the slaughter of the fugitives was terrible! They mostly hurried towards the river; "and at the entry of the bridge of Najera there was a hideous shedding of blood, and many a man slain and drowned, for divers leaped into the water, which was deep." At the bridge of Navaretta there was also a choke, and great loss of life; and there fell the Grand Prior of St. James and the Grand Master of the Knights of Calatrava. "The water that ran by Navaret," adds Froissard, "was of the colour of red, with the blood of men and horses that were there slain." King Henry's lodgings were pillaged, and therein were found great plenty of jewels, and rich vessels of gold and silver; but he, knowing that a terrible death awaited him if taken by the merciless Pedro, had escaped by a safe and secret route. Pedro, on the field, deliberately murdered with his own hand Inigo Lopez de Orosco, a noble Castilian, who had been taken prisoner by a knight of Gascony; and he repeatedly said, "If the bastard be not killed, the business is but half complete." The great Sir John Chandos had on this clay a narrow escape. Having pressed too far among the enemy, he was surrounded and felled to the earth, where he was grappled with by a huge Castilian of noted prowess, named Martin Fenant, and would have been slain had he not bethought himself of a knife that was in the bosom of his surcoat. This he plunged repeatedly into the back and ribs of Martin as he lay above him; then he turned him over on his back, and started up just as his followers came to his rescue. The dagger which knights employed in these close and deadly struggles was named, somewhat inaptly, the "poniard of mercy." The Black Prince would have thought the battle dearly won had Chandos perished, even though the number of slain had been no more than the incredibly small amount stated by Froissard, as four knights and some forty others. Of the four knights, "two were Gascons, the third an Almayne, and the fourth an Englishman." Of the Spaniards and French, 560 men-at-arms lay dead on the field, and between 7,000 and 8,000 more were destroyed or drowned in the flight and pursuit.

Many prisoners were taken; the principal of these, to quote the "History of Pedro,"; were "Don Sancho de Castilla, base brother of Pedro; Du Guesclin; the Marshal Arnauld d'Endreghen; the Begue de Vilaine; the Count of Denia, of the royal line of Arragon; Philip de Castro, brother-in-law of Henry; Pedro Lope de Ayala, the historian, and many lords." The number of prisoners of rank was about 2,000, whereof 200 were French, and not a few were Scots.

The next day, Sunday, the remorseless Pedro craved leave to put all these prisoners to death; a measure to which the Black Prince would by no means consent, and represented to him in strong terms that if he did not relax the severity of his temper the victory was useless. However, he would not be satisfied until the Commander of St. James, Garci Jofre, son of the Admiral of Castile, and Gomez Carillo de Quintana, were slaughtered, the last-named at the door of his tent.

All Castile now submitted to Pedro, who would never forgive the Prince of Wales for his clemency to the prisoners. He withheld the stipulated pay of the English troops; thus young Edward, though he had finished his perilous enterprise with glory, had soon cause to repent that he had undertaken it in the cause of a monster. He sold his plate and jewels to feed his brave soldiers, but they perished fast by hunger and sickness; and his own health being impaired hopelessly by the climate,, he was compelled to retreat into Guienne. The tyrannies of Pedro drove the Castilians speedily again to arms. He had no longer the sword of the Black Prince to rely upon. Defeated at Toledo, within a year after the victory at Najera, he took refuge in a castle, where he was captured and brought before his brother, Henry, by the Beque de Vilaine, and then ensued a scene of horror. The brothers were at last face to face. A few words of scorn and reproach passed between them, and then they rushed on each other like wild beasts. Pedro drew a secret dagger; it was wrenched from his hand by the Viscount" de Roquebertin, and placed in the grasp of his brother, who stabbed him to death. From that moment Henry was sole monarch of Castile and Leon, the crown of which he transmitted to his posterity.

Najera proved a fatal field to the great and gallant Prince Edward, who was soon after obliged to return to England, where he wasted and died, in his forty-sixth year, and was interred at Canterbury, where may still be seen, above the altar-tomb wheron his effigy lies, some of his armour, his shield, with the fleur-de-lis and lions, his surcoat, now faded to a dusky brown, his helmet, and gauntlets, the same perhaps which he wore when in prayer and battle on the field of Najera, in Castile.

SEA-FIGHT, 1378 - OTTERBURNE, OR CHEVY CHASE, 1388

A FTER THE accession of the Black Prince's son to
the throne, as Richard II, the naval affairs of England
were so much neglected that most of the towns along
the coast of the Channel were pillaged and burned by the French.
At length a little fleet was fitted out, under Richard Fitzalan,
Earl of Arundel, and William de Montacute, Earl of Salisbury,
with orders to take possession of Cherbourg, which the King of
Navarre had promised to deliver to the English. On the sea they
were attacked by the Spaniards, who still resented the battle of
Najera, but were beaten off; and the two earls put a garrison into
Cherbourg, thus giving England an opening into Normandy, as
Calais did into Picardy.

In his latter years King Edward III had most bitterly repented
the neglect of naval affairs. During the long-continued hostility
with Scotland that marked the reign of David II, the Scottish
ships of war plundered the merchants of England, and made
repeated descents upon her coast; and not unfrequently her
ships, when at anchor or in harbour, were cut out in sight of the
people. The commerce of England suffered severely from these
attacks; and Tytler quotes from *"Rotuli Scotiæ"* a remarkable
order addressed by Edward III to his admirals and naval captains,
complaining in bitter terms "of their pusillanimous conduct in
permitting the united fleets of the Scots, French, and Flemings
to capture and destroy the ships of England in the very sight of
his own navy."

While the two earls were with the fleet at Cherbourg, an
opulent Scottish merchant, named John Mercer, who resided
in France, and was greatly esteemed by Charles the Wise,

had been captured on the sea by some Northumbrians, and carried prisoner into Scarborough. In revenge for this, his son, a bold and enterprising mariner, fitted out a fleet of Scottish, French, and Castilian ships, with which he attacked and burned Scarborough, and carried off the ships that lay there. Thence he sailed to the Channel, the coast of which he continued to scour with impunity, and captured many richly-laden prizes bound for London, thereby inflicting great damage upon English commerce. The losses he occasioned the merchants, caused loud complaints against the Duke of Lancaster, who had undertaken to protect England by sea, but as yet had failed to do so.

At length John Philpot, a wealthy and public-spirited merchant of London, on his own responsibility, fitted out a squadron, of vessels, put 1,000 soldiers on board, and sailed in quest of Mercer. After a little time he came up with him in the Channel, and a severe battle ensued, of which Walsingham gives us no other details than that Philpot proved victorious, and took all Mercer's fleet, together with many of the prizes he had captured. The Scottish mariner was brought in triumph to London, where the victor obtained the applause of the people; but the Regents resented that a private individual should have undertaken such an expedition without their consent. The patriotic Philpot, however, made so able a defence of himself "that he was dismissed without further trouble."

The naval power of England remained at the same low ebb during the reigns of Richard II and Henry IV; and hence it is that in the annals of those times we read of repeated projects of invasion by the French, and of constant depredations on the coast of England by their squadrons.

OTTERBURNE, OR CHEVY CHASE

A projected attack on England by land and sea from France and

Scotland ended only in drawing an English army into the latter country, with fire and sword, as far as Perth and Dundee; and after some ten years of war and ravage, with alternate; truces and negotiations, was fought the battle of Otterburne, perhaps one of the most splendid encounters in the annals of chivalry.

England was now rent, as Scotland had so often been, by internal dissensions, the result of weakness in the unfortunate Richard II, and the ambition of his nobles; hence the Scottish barons of King Robert II deemed the opportunity most favourable to retaliate upon her for past injuries. A preliminary meeting was held by them at Jedburgh; and having there made all their arrangements, they appointed a muster-place, and keeping all their plans secret from the king and his councillors, they separated, each to prepare his vassals and followers.

The village of Yetholm, not far from Jedburgh, and situated at the base of the Cheviot Mountains, was the next trysting-place; and there on a day in the middle of August, 1388, came the Earls of Douglas, Moray, and Fife, Sir James Lindesay, of Crawford, and other barons, with a following of 1,200 men-at-arms and 40,000 infantry. On the other side of the border, the English lords, who by minstrels and heralds - alike privileged spies - had been duly informed of this unexpected muster (the largest Scotland had seen for some years), were far from being idle, and began to prepare for resistance, and actually dispatched a gentleman to Yetholm to discover the objects and strength of the Scots. This gentleman, or squire, as Froissard calls him, disguised as a groom, had the hardihood to enter the church where the Scottish chiefs were holding council, and learned the whole of their plans; but when he returned to the place where he had left his horse tied to a tree, he found that it had been stolen, and, afraid to make any inquiries concerning it, he set off towards England on foot (Buchanan says, "in his boots, spurs, and riding-suit"), but this very caution led to his detection.

"I have witnessed many wonderful things," said a Scottish knight to a friend, as they stood at the church door, "but what I now see surpasses any. Yonder man has lost his horse, and yet makes no inquiry about it. On my troth, I doubt much if he belongs to us. Let us after him, and see whether I am right or not."

His confused and contradictory answers confirmed their suspicions; he was made a prisoner, interrogated, and threatened with instant death if he failed to reveal the intentions and force of his countrymen; and from his confession the Scottish leaders learned that the English did not yet deem their troops numerous enough for battle; but had resolved to await the inroad of the Scots, and then to make a counter-invasion of Scotland. "Should you march through Cumberland," added the unlucky spy, "they will take the road through Berwick to Dunbar and Edinburgh; should you take the other way, then they will march by Carlisle, and enter your country by these mountains."

The Scottish nobles were in the highest spirits at this intelligence, says Froissard, "and considered their success as certain now that they knew the disposition of the enemy. They

The village of Yetholm.

held council as to their mode of procedure, and the wisest and most accustomed to arms, such as Sir Archibald Douglas, the Earl of Fife, Sir Alexander Ramsay, Sir John Sinclair, and Sir James Lindesay, were the speakers;" and, to frustrate the object of the English, it was resolved to cross the border in two divisions, by the Eastern and Western Marches.

Accordingly one division, the largest, led by the Earl of Fife, the king's second son, and others, began to march through Liddesdale towards Carlisle, while the other, and smallest, consisting of 300 men-at-arms and 2,000 infantry, led by the young and fiery Earl of Douglas - the rival of Piercy - by a swift and rapid march, pushed on through Northumberland without molesting the inhabitants; but as soon as the bishopric of Durham was reached the plundering began, and the smoke of the blazing villages acquainted the English leaders that the Scots had crossed the border. Douglas was permitted to ravage the whole of that beautiful and populous district without opposition, as the English supposed that he was but the vanguard of the entire army. After destroying the country to the gates of Durham, Douglas returned by the way of Newcastle, which was garrisoned by the brave Sir Henry Piercy, surnamed Hotspur. His force was too slender to attack Douglas in the field; but the English knights frequently dashed out from their defences to break a lance with the Scottish, and many noble deeds of chivalry were there done. In one of these hostile meetings, Douglas and Hotspur encountered hand to hand. After a long combat - for in arms, strength, and almost in years, they were equal - the latter was discomfited, and his lance with its silken pennon was wrested from him. Raising himself in his stirrups, Douglas shook it triumphantly aloft, exclaiming -

"I shall carry this to Scotland, and place it on the highest tower of my castle of Dalkeith, so that it may be seen from afar."

"By heaven, Earl of Douglas," cried Piercy, "thou shalt not

even bear it out of Northumberland! Thou shalt never have my pennon in Scotland to brag of."

"Well," replied Douglas, "your pennon shall this night be placed before the door of my tent - come and take it if you can."

Such was the defiance that led to the battle of Otterburne, better known in song and story as "the battle of Chevy Chase;" for Douglas continued his march up the Tyne, and when he encamped at night he stuck the lance of Hotspur in the ground before his tent, never doubting that its gallant owner would come to redeem his pledge.

The armour of this period partook of the extravagant modes of the age. Plate was soon so completely worn that the gussets of chain at the joints and the chain apron were all that remained of the old mail of the tenth century. The jupon and military girdle were still worn, and visored bascinets were sometimes used, with the ventaille fashioned like the beak of a bird; while the bascinet itself was often encircled by a band or fillet of ermine, or border of beautiful workmanship. Milan was now the grand emporium for equipping the chivalry of Europe. Heraldic crests on the helmet are said to have not been generally used in Scotland for a hundred years after they were worn in England by all men of rank; and they excited surprise in the Scots in the very year of Otterburne. In 1385 the Scottish Parliament ordained that every Scottish and French soldier in their service should wear a white St. Andrew's cross on his breast and back, which, if his surcoat was white, was to be embroidered on a division of black cloth. According to a book called the "Lamp of Lothian," the armour of Douglas and his squire took a year to temper and make.

Henry Piercy was born in 1366, and was now in his twenty-second year. Douglas was older, as Froissard, who, about the year named, spent fifteen days at the castle of Dalkeith, speaks of him as "a promising youth."

Piercy's evident desire to attack Douglas that night, and regain his lance with its pennon, was overruled by the English leaders, who were still under the impression that the whole army of the Scottish barons was close at hand, and that the earl sought to draw them into an ambush. Douglas waited some time, expecting an attack; and then resuming his homeward march, after destroying the tower of Ponteland, he arrived on the second day at the hamlet of Otterburne, in Redesdale, about thirty miles from Newcastle. There he halted, for the double purpose of reducing a strong castle which stood there, and of giving Hotspur an opportunity for regaining his lance, especially as the latter had now mustered a far superior force. Douglas pitched his camp on the banks of the Reed Water. A marsh flanked him on one side, on the other was a small hill covered by leafy timber; in his front he placed all his wagons and carts, sumpter horses, and so forth, in charge of the sutlers and drivers, to guard against surprise. Having spent the day in skirmishing with the people in the castle, the Scots retired to their camp; while Hotspur, having now discovered that the forces of his rival in arms were but a small detached column, was coming on with all speed, at the head of 6,000 men-at-arms (horse and man all sheathed in steel) and 8,000 infantry.

Froissard, so picturesquely "minute in his descriptions, tells us that it was after sunset when Piercy came in sight of the little Scottish camp. It was a sweet moonlight evening - the last one of July - clear and bright, with a soft fresh breeze, though the past day-had been warm. Most of the Scots, fatigued by the assault of the castle, had taken their evening meal, and then lain down to rest. Earl Douglas and their other leaders had taken off their armour, and were at supper in their gowns and doublets, when the gleam of spears and mail was seen amid the grassy glen, and the cry of "A Piercy! a Piercy!" rang upon the still air, while Hotspur came on with great fury. Buchanan says that the moon shone so brightly that her light was equal to that of day, and that "To your arms!" was the shout of the Scots. The English men-at-arms fell with sword and axe upon the barricade of wagons, which was defended by the camp-followers, and thus gave those in camp time to arm and get into their ranks; but they had to accoutre in such haste that the armour of Douglas in many places was unclasped, and the Earl of Moray had to fight all night bareheaded, without his helmet.

Earl Douglas now gave his banner to his natural son, a mere youth, named Archibald Douglas, ancestor of the family of Cavers, hereditary Sheriffs of Teviotdale, by whom it is still preserved; and, charging him "to defend it to the last drop of his blood," instead of waiting within camp to receive a closer assault of the enemy, drew off his troops, and sweeping in silence round the wooded hill, fell on the flank of the English while they were entangled in the marsh which bordered on the camp.

Hotspur, who had now discovered his mistake, drew back his force to firmer ground, and received the attack of the enemy with great gallantry. If the English were somewhat fatigued by a long and hot day's march, they were superior in number to the Scots, "and in the temper of their armour and weapons." And now the hand-to-hand conflict raged for some hours with equal fury and ferocity, till the moon suddenly became obscured by a cloud so dark that, as Buchanan states, "friend could not be discerned from foe; whereupon they rested a space to recover breath." When the moon shone forth again, the conflict was resumed over the dead and dying, and the Scots, who fought against treble their number, began slowly to give way; till Douglas, whose standard was nearly lost, wielding a battle-axe with both hands, and followed by a few of his household, and his most faithful friends, Robert Hart and Simon Glendonwyn, hewed a passage amid the thickest of the enemy, till, being

Hotspur's night attack.

completely isolated from his men, he was borne to the earth and mortally wounded in the head and thigh. The first-named wound would seem to corroborate the old ballad, which asserts that, like the Earl of Moray, he had entered the action in haste, without his helmet. "The Scottish spearmen were about giving way," to quote the "Lamp of Lothian," "when John Swinton, a brave knight, instead of pushing forward with his spear, raised it aloft, and, with herculean strength, smashed the shafts of the foremost rank of the enemy. He did this with such effect that the panic was fatal."

The disaster to Douglas was unknown to the Scots for a time, till the tide of battle turned; and on the English being forced to give way, the spot where the great earl lay was cleared by dint of sword and spear, and Sir James Lindesay, Sir John and Sir Walter Sinclair were the first to discover him as he was bleeding to death. Near him lay his banner, the bearer of which had fallen. His chaplain, William Lundie, afterwards archdeacon of North Berwick, who had fought during the whole battle by his side, was still there, armed with a curtal-axe, and bestriding his body to protect him from further harm.

"How fares it with you, cousin?" asked Sir John Sinclair.

"But so so," replied the earl, in a weak voice; "yet, God be thanked, few of my ancestors have died in chambers or in beds. There has long been a prophecy that 'a dead Douglas should win a field,' and I trust it shall now be fulfilled. My heart sinks - I am dying. Do you, Walter, and you, John Sinclair, raise my banner and war-cry; but tell neither friend nor foe that Douglas is lying here."

These were his last words. Buchanan says they covered his body with a mantle, erected the banner, and shouted, "A Douglas! a Douglas!" A fresh onslaught was made on the English. Hotspur, who was wounded, was captured by the Earl of Moray, and his troops losing heart, gave way and took to flight; so that, literally, the dead Douglas won the field. Scarcely a man of note among the English escaped either death or captivity; 1,860 of their men-at-arms were slain, and more than 1,000 were wounded. Froissard, who received his account of the battle from both the English and Scottish knights who were engaged in it, says in his chronicle, "Of all the battles that have been described in this history, great and small, this was the best fought and the most severe; for there was not a man, knight or squire, who did not acquit himself gallantly hand to hand with his enemy, without either stay or faint-heartedness." He adds that they all agreed that it was one of the most obstinate battles ever fought. In his "Annales," Sir James Balfour states that the only Scots "of quality" who fell were Sir Robert Heriot, Sir John Touris of Inverleith, and Sir William Lundin, who died of his wounds three days after the battle.

On the following day the Bishop of Durham, hearing of Piercy's defeat, arrived at Otterburne in hot haste, with 10,000 men, to cut off the retreat of the Scots; but finding them strongly intrenched, under the Earl of Moray, he deemed it more prudent to let them retreat home without molestation. In solemn procession, the body of Douglas was borne to the abbey church of Melrose, and laid in the tomb of his forefathers, above which his banner was hung. Among the noble prisoners carried into Scotland were, besides Hotspur, his brother, Sir Ralph Piercy, the Seneschal of York, Sir Ralph Langley, Sir Robert Ogle, Sir John Lilburn, Sir John Copeland, Sir Thomas Walsingham, Sir John Felton, Sir Thomas Abingdon, and half of the chivalry of the northern shires. Froissard highly applauds the courtesy shown by the Scots to their prisoners, and adds "that both nations were not less deserving of praise for their gentleness after a battle than for their courage during the conflict;" from which we may suppose that much of the savage rancour infused in these wars by the ferocious policy of Edward I was passing away.

While this brilliant field was fought in Redesdale, the main body of the Scottish army was simply occupied in the devastation of the western counties of England; and Andrew Wynton records that its leader, the Earl of Fife, heard of it with envy, for the wealth that accrued from the ransom of the prisoners was the most remarkable that had occurred since Bannockburn. Froissard estimates it at 200,000 francs.

For his ransom to the Lord Montgomerie, Hotspur built the castle of Penrose, in Ayrshire, belonging to the future Earls of Eglinton; and the King of Scotland redeemed Ralph Piercy from Sir Henry Preston, of the family of Craigmillar, by granting him certain lands and baronies in Aberdeenshire.

Such was the field of Chevy Chase, the story of which so roused the heroic blood of Sir Philip Sidney that he wrote, "I never heard the old song of Piercy and Douglas, that I found not my heart moved more thereby than with the sound of a trumpet; and yet it is sung but by some blind crowder, with no rougher voice than rude style."

HOMILDON, 1402 - SHREWSBURY, 1403

HOMILDON

IN ENGLAND and in Scotland, the earliest military force - apart from clanship in the latter country - arose from the feudal system, service in war being performed under that tenure: the greater vassals holding immediately of the respective crowns, under that obligation; and the inferior vassals from the others, on the express condition of appearing in arms under their lord's standard, whenever he should require their services. This was enforced by the right of confiscation, or resumption of the lands granted under the condition, although the usual punishment was a pecuniary fine. Every possessor of a knight's fee in England, where there were more than 60,000, was obliged to furnish one soldier for the king's service during forty days in each year.

So early as the reign of Edward II, we find a chirurgeon for every 1,900 men. His pay was four-pence per diem. Henry V had one surgeon and twelve assistants with his army; and they rank thus in his military code, drawn up at Manse: "Soldiers, shoemakers, taylors, barbers, physicians, and washerwomen."

A tax was first levied under Elizabeth for the support of "maimed soldiers and mariners;" but so early as the days of which we are writing grants of money were occasionally made by the sovereigns of England to men wounded in action. Thus, in the ordinances of Edward IV, we find an allowance of four marks per annum to John Sclatter, a private soldier of foot, who had lost a hand at the battle of Wakefield; and ten pounds per annum to another, for gallantry at the battle of Sherborne.

A Scottish war being the first undertaking of Henry IV on his accession, the old rivalry and hostility between the great border lords, Piercy and Douglas, flamed out anew, and the flower of the Lothians fell in battle at Nisbet Muir. Incensed by that disaster, Archibald, fourth Earl of Douglas, afterwards a Marshal of France, collected 10,000 men, and accompanied by Murdoch Stuart, eldest son of the Duke of Albany, the Earls of Moray and Angus, together with Fergus Macdowal, Lord of Galloway, at the head of the fierce Celtic clans of the southern Highlands, entered England, and, in the usual fashion, laid waste all the beautiful border land to the gates of Newcastle. At this crisis Henry IV, whose wanton invasion of Scotland in the preceeding year had drawn the present expedition on himself, was engaged in suppressing the Welsh insurrection under Owen Glendower; but he had left the charge of the English frontier in the able hands of the Earl of Northumberland and his son, the gallant Hotspur. These experienced leaders, together with the Earl of March, who was well skilled in border warfare, and was a Scottish malcontent or refugee, collected a powerful army; and resolved to intercept the Scots when on their homeward march, encumbered by spoil and with herds of cattle, and while they seemed lulled into security by the apparent fear of the English borderers a policy which was completely successful.

On his northern march, the Earl of Douglas had reached Wooler ere he received intelligence that Hotspur, at the head of a strong army, was barring the way to Scotland, and advancing to attack him. On this he immediately took up a position on an eminence called Homildon Hill; and though the high courage of Douglas, like that of all the men of his race, is unquestionable, his errors as a leader were many and grave. The position he chose was completely commanded by several other eminences, especially by one directly in front of his line; and of it, by the most singular fatality, he quietly permitted the English, on the

7th of May, 1402, to possess themselves, and form in order of battle. The dense ranks of the Scottish spearmen were thus exposed to the point-blank arrows of the English archers, who composed a very large portion of Piercy's army, while the old movement inaugurated by Bruce - their dispersion by a charge of light horse - was never thought of. Too well might the archers of England boast that each of them carried twelve. Scotsmen's lives in his belt. With his characteristic impetuosity, Hotspur proposed an immediate charge on the Scottish spears at the head of his mounted men-at-arms; but the renegade Earl of March, seizing the reins of his bridle, suggested that the archers should first empty their quivers. Marching to the front, in obedience to this evil genius of his country, the English archers poured in their volleys "thick as hail upon their foes, whose ranks," says an ancient writer, "were so closely wedged together that a breath of air could scarcely penetrate their files, making it impossible for them to wield their weapons." The Scottish pikemen, most of whom were clad in light armour, fell in hundreds over each other; and many of their knights, who still adhered to the old-fashioned chain-mail, found it no defence against the deadly English shafts. They fell fast from their horses; and these, wounded, ungovernable, their breasts and flanks bristling with blood-stained arrows, galloped madly to and fro, trampling the dead and the dying together. By the statutes of Robert I, every peasant in Scotland who possessed a cow was compelled to procure a bow and sheaf of twenty - four arrows, or a spear and coat of mail; but with the former weapon they never excelled. Now, at Homildon, the northern bowmen attempted to place the fight on a more equal footing; but, distracted by the confusion and carnage around them, their arrows either fell short of the English ranks, or their flights were ineffectual. It was when the Scots were in this sore extremity that Sir John Swinton of that ilk, an aged knight of distinguished valour, exclaimed: "Why stand we thus,to be shot down like deer? Where is our wonted courage? Are we to be still, as if our hands were nailed to our lances? Follow me, and let us at least sell our lives as dearly as we can!"

This brave proposition won him the admiration of Adam Gordon, a young border noble, who had long been at deadly feud with Swinton. Leaping from his horse, he knelt before him, and, in the grand spirit of that chivalric age, he begged forgiveness for his past hate, and to obtain the honour of knighthood from his sword - "For from a hand more noble than thine, Swinton, can I never receive the honour."

Swinton acceded to the request, and embraced his former foe. The two knights then remounted, and at the head of one hundred lances flung themselves at full speed upon the foe; but being totally unsupported, the whole of this little band and its two leaders were overpowered and slain. Earl Douglas now

Saddle, helmet, and shield of Henry V in Westminster Abbey.

made a final effort to retrieve the day, by making, when the movement was too late, a desperate charge at the head of his men-at-arms, with axe and lance - a step which hastened his own overthrow.

Retiring regularly on their cavalry, the English still continued that deadly rain of arrows under which the advancing Scots began to waver, and at last to break and retreat. Then, with a shout, the archers, relinquishing their bows for the short axe and daggers, rushed among them, mingled with the cavalry, and slew or captured many of the invaders. By them the battle was entirely won; of the men-at-arms under Piercy, scarcely one drew a sword or laid a lance in rest. The loss of the victors was very trifling, but that of the Scots was great. One author (Tindal, in his Notes to Rapin) estimates it at 10,000 men, which is absurd; but 1,500 of them were certainly drowned in the Tweed.

Douglas lost an eye, and was otherwise wounded in four places. Sir John Swinton; Sir Adam Gordon, of that ilk and Huntly; Sir John Livingstone, of Callender; Sir Alexander Ramsay, of Dalhousie; Sir Walter Scott, of Murdieston; Sir Walter Sinclair, and many other knights and esquires, lay dead on the field: while among the prisoners of Hotspur were the Earl of Douglas; Murdoch, son of Robert the Regent Duke of Albany; Stuart of Lorn; the Master of Dalkeith; Logan of Restalrig - in all some eighty nobles and knights, belonging to the first families in Scotland, a most unfortunate capture, as they ultimately proved, for Henry IV of England.

More than ever did the result of that 7th of May prove that the flower of England's feudal infantry were her archers. Made either from yew, ash, hazel, -or elm, the bow was put into the hands of every English boy at the age of seven, and it ceased not to furnish him with sport and occupation till years deprived his arm of strength and his eye of skill; and from the Conquest down to the introduction of the musket, the use of this weapon was enforced by the English legislature. The following is the description of an English archer, as given by Ralph Smithe: -

"Captains and officers should be skilful of that most noble weapon, and to see that their soldiers, according to their draught and strength, have good bows, well nocked, well strynged, everie strynge whippe in their nock, and in the middles rubbed with wax; braser and shooting-glove; some spare strynges as aforesaid. Everie man one shefe of arrows with a case of leather, defensible against the rayne; and in the same foure-and-twenty arrows, whereof eight of them should be lighter than the residue, to gall or astonye the enemy with the hail-shot of light arrowes. Let everie man have a brigandine, or little cote of plate; a skull (cap), or hufkin; a maul of, lead, five foot in length; and a pike, and the same hanging by his side, with a hook and dagger. Being thus furnished, teach them by masters to march, shoote, and r'etyre, keeping their faces to the enemy. Some time put them in great nowmbers, as to battell appertayneth, and thus use them oftentymes till they be perfecte; for those men in battell or skirmish cannot be spared.

A royal and more recent author says, "A first-rate English archer who in a single minute was unable to draw and discharge his bow twelve times, with a range of 250 yards, and who in these twelve shots once missed his man, was very lightly esteemed."

SHREWSBURY

Henry IV received the tidings of the victory at Homildon with the liveliest satisfaction; but, in consequence of his own pride and imprudence, it led to events which placed his throne in imminent peril. By the laws of chivalry, all captives taken in war belonged then entirely to the victor, who might ransom or retain them at his pleasure. In violation of this law, Henry, on the 22nd

September, 1402, dispatched from Winchester a prohibition to the Earl of Northumberland "to dispose of the Scotch prisoners taken at the battell of Humbledon," either by ransom or otherwise, till he received further instructions on the subject. The secret of this order was that Henry had certain designs on Scotland, which the detention of so many noble captives would greatly facilitate; but it was felt as an insult and injustice by Hotspur and his father. To soften them, Henry, in the plentitude of his folly and arrogance, conferred on the former by letters-patent the Scottish earldom of Douglas. As this would require to be won and held by the sword, it was a kind of joke that Piercy's temper could ill brook, especially as he had another ground of resentment against the king, in his refusal to ransom Sir Edward Mortimer, their kinsman, from Owen Glendower, because he was meanly jealous of the superior rights of the house of Mortimer. So the Piercys resolved to dethrone the ungrateful monarch whom they had helped to place on the throne, and to exalt in his place the young Earl of March. For this purpose they formed a coalition which seemed almost irresistible. They granted the Earl of Douglas his liberty, on condition that he and all his friends and followers should join them; and they admitted into this strange confederacy Glendower, who promised to join them with at least 10,000 mountaineers when they drew near Wales; and they proposed to divide England among them, as if it were already escheated property.

Mortimer, on behalf of his nephew, the Earl of March, was to obtain all the country from the Trent and the Severn to the southeast limits of the kingdom; the Piercys were to have all the land from the Trent to the borders, while the district north of the Severn was to belong to Owen Glendower. Save in the case of the latter, these conspirators were uninspired by any patriotism; all was grasping selfishness and a desire for vengeance. As for Douglas and the other Scots, they served Hotspur to pay their ransom; and to fight against the King of England was to fight the common enemy of their country.

Fortunately for England, the talents and activity of Henry IV were equal to this great crisis, and he had at hand a body of troops with which he had been intending to act against the Scots; and with them he instantly marched westward, by messengers directing all his faithful subjects to join him. Mortimer by this time had married the daughter of Owen Glendower, and informed the more trusty of his own retainers that he had joined the Welsh chief in a righteous quarrel, with the view of winning the crown again for King Richard, whom he alleged to be concealed among the Scots; and if he was dead, for the Earl of March. On this Hotspur had hastened to North Wales, where he possessed considerable influence, accompanied by Douglas and the Scottish knights; and his uncle, the Earl of Worcester, who was Lieutenant of South Wales, joined him with all the forces he could muster. The archers of Cheshire, a race of men devoted to the late king, answered his summons to a man; but

The battlefield of Shrewsbury.

Henry had marched into Shrewsbury with all his followers, at the very time that the glitter of the insurgents' armour could be descried from its picturesque old walls, and ere a junction had been formed by the troops of the fiery and impetuous Hotspur and those of the wild, gloomy, and enthusiastic Glendower. The former, disappointed by this, but not discouraged, drew up his troops at Haytleyfield, four miles distant from Shrewsbury, and prepared for a battle that was to prove one of the most severe and sanguinary in the civil wars of England.

In the evening, Hotspur, who was then in his thirty-sixth year, and in the zenith of his military fame, Governor of Berwick, and Warden of the East Marches of England, sent a manifesto to Henry. In that document he renounced his allegiance, set the monarch at defiance, and, in the name of his father and uncle, enumerated all the grievances of which he alleged the nation had to complain. He upbraided him with the perjury of which he had been guilty, when, on landing at Ravenspur, he had sworn upon the gospels that he had no other intention than to recover the Duchy of Lancaster, and would ever remain a faithful subject to King Richard, whom he had first dethroned and then murdered. He charged him again with perjury, in loading the nation with heavy taxes; he reproached him with tampering in the Parliamentary elections - acts which had himself before imputed to Richard, and made one reason for his dethronment.

This manifesto filled the heart of the king with rancorous fury, and the next day, the 21st of July, 1403, saw the adverse armies, each mustering about 14,000 men, ready to engage among the fields and upland slopes, in view of the people of Shrewsbury. So doubtful was Henry of the result, that he sent the abbot of that place with certain proposals of peace, which were rejected by the advice of Worcester.

"Then," cried Henry, "banners, advance!" and the air began to resound with the adverse war-cries of "St. George!" and

"Esperance, Piercy!" - the latter being the motto of Hotspur, whose crest was a lion - and the archers on each side began to discharge their arrows with the usual murderous effect. Piercy and Douglas, who a year before had been enemies and rivals, were now comrades and friends; and, with thirty chosen knights, rode side by side, as they hewed a way for themselves into the very heart of Henry's host. Douglas had sworn that the King of England should that day die by his hand, and he sought him all over the field. But Henry, acting under the advice of the Scottish Earl of March, had prudently changed his armour, and, as a simple man-at-arms, was doing his duty elsewhere, and had his horse killed under him. He had several gentlemen, however, dressed in the royal insignia of England, and the sword of the one-eyed Douglas rendered this honour fatal to most of them, Sir William Blount among others.

"I marvel to see so many kings rising again!" exclaimed the bewildered Scot. "Where do they all come from?"

Hotspur and he bore all before them for a time. The king's guards were dispersed, his standard beaten to the ground, and the Prince of Wales received a wound on the face. Disappointed in their expectations of slaying the king, Hotspur and Douglas were cutting a passage back through those who had closed upon their rear, when the former fell, neither by the hand of the king or Harry of Monmouth, but by a random arrow, which pierced his brain at the very moment he had lifted the ventaille of his helmet for air, or to issue an order. This decided the victory, for with him fell the courage and the cause of his followers, who now dispersed in all directions. In this unhappy strife there fell 2,300 gentlemen alone. Those of the greatest distinction lost under the banner of the king were the Earl of Stafford, Sir Hugh Shirley, Sir Nicholas Gansel, Sir Hugh Mortimer, Sir John Massey, Sir William Blount, and Sir John Calverley. About 6,000 private men fell, of these two-thirds were followers of

Hotspur. All the Scottish auxiliaries perished, save Douglas and the Earl of Worcester. The former was wounded in his knee, and was released with the courtesy due to his rank; but the latter was beheaded at Shrewsbury, and his skull was placed upon London Bridge. Boethius asserts that Douglas slew certainly four that were armed on all points like King Henry, who, according to Walsingham, killed thirty-six men with his own hand. The body of the gallant Hotspur was buried with his permission; afterwards altering his mind, he barbarously had it exhumed, dismembered, and placed on poles in the highways.

The Earl of Northumberland afterwards fled to Scotland. Returning, after five years of wandering, peril, and penury, he was slain at Tadcaster, in Yorkshire.

AGINCOURT, 1415

THE EMPTY title of "King of France" was claimed until recent years by our monarchs; but Harry of Monmouth was the only English sovereign who ever really deserved the name. Taking advantage of the civil war which convulsed France, after his accession he revived the claim of Edward III, and demanded the fulfilment of the Treaty of Bretigny. In derision of this, there came from the Dauphin for answer a bale of tennis-balls, as a gentle hint that the young King of England was fitter for such sports than the rougher game of war. Stung by this insult, Henry V prepared for battle. The Duke of Bedford was appointed Regent; the royal jewels were pawned, loans were raised, and the great barons were called to arms: and though some delays arose in consequence of a plot in favour of the Earl of March - a plot for which Lord Scroop and Richard of Cambridge had to die - a fleet bore Henry with an army 30,000 strong (6,000 were horse) from Southampton to the mouth of the Seine. In five weeks he reduced the strong fortress of Harfleur, on the right bank of the river; and then, with an army reduced to nearly half its original number by sickness, wounds, and desertion, he formed the bold resolution of cutting a passage to Calais by the same route as that pursued by Edward III when he marched his troops to victory. This daring march of a hundred miles, through every species of opposition and danger, began on the 8th of October. The English moved in three columns, with cavalry on their flanks. But Henry found the bridges of the Somme broken down, and the fords rendered perilous by lines of pointed stakes, till, after some delay, one undefended place was discovered near St. Quentin. He crossed rapidly, and marched upon Calais; while the Constable of France quietly awaited his approach at the village of Agincourt, on the left of the road from Abbeville to St. Omer.

It is strange that in all these operations we hear nothing more of cannon, which the English certainly possessed at home; for when Henry besieged Berwick, in 1405, we are told that a shot from one great gun so shattered a tower that the gates were instantly thrown open by the alarmed garrison. Hand-guns were not yet invented, and the bow was still the king of English weapons. In those days, when men-at-arms encountered each other the slaughter was seldom great: many were unhorsed, when they lay helpless until assisted to rise again; and in hot weather many were suffocated or choked in blood if their visors were not unclasped. Those among them who perished by sword-cut or lance-thrust were few in comparison to the slaughter made when they found an opening in a square of infantry, or

View of Harfleur.

174

came suddenly on unprotected archers. Hence we see that at Bannockburn the yeomanry of the English army perished almost to a man under the lances of the Scottish knights; at Flodden the Scottish bill-men were cut to pieces by the English men-at-arms; and at Homildon the Scots, and at Cressy and Poictiers the French, were destroyed chiefly by the volleys of the English archers.

In the English military equipment of the time of Henry V, a plume in the apex of the helmet was a leading feature, and the form of the helmet itself was remarkably beautiful, with an orle or chaplet around it. The breastplates had become globular, and the steel gorget was replacing the ancient camail which had hitherto protected the throat. Hanging sleeves of rich cloth were sometimes worn with the armour; the lance-rests were hooks just below the right breast; two-handed swords with heavy blades were introduced at this time; and a pole-axe was usually carried by commanders in the field. Monstrelet, in his Chronicles, describes the English archers as being for the most part without armour, and in jackets, with their hose loose, with-. out hats or caps, and often barefooted. Their hatchets or swords hung at their girdle. St. Remy says that they were not bareheaded, and that many of them wore caps of *cuir bouilli*, or boiled leather, and others of wicker-work, crossed over with bars of iron. He was present at the glorious field of Agincourt, and tells us how young Henry of England, at break of day, heard three masses in succession clad in all his armour save his helmet and emblazoned surcoat. After the last mass, they "brought him the armour for his head, which was a very handsome bascinet with a baviere, upon which he had a very rich crown of gold circled over like an imperial crown." If this means with arches, it is the first instance of an English monarch wearing a closed crown.

Another historian says, "His helmet was of polished steel,

surmounted by a crown sparkling with jewels, and on his surcoat were emblazoned the arms of England and of France."

The night before Agincourt was dark and rainy, and to the toil-worn English it was one of hope and fear, for 100,000 French lay there before them; thus the odds against them were as seven to one. Amid the darkness of the October, night, and the sheets of descending rain, they could see the whole landscape glittering with the watch-fires of the French; and frequent bursts of their laughter and merriment were borne on the passing wind, from those who were grouped about these fires or their banners, as they fixed the ransom of the English king and his wealthy barons. As for the common soldiers, they were all to be put to the sword, without mercy. Confident in their overwhelming numbers, they never conceived the possibility of defeat; yet could they forget that they were posted within but a few miles of Cressy?

As men who had staked their lives and the warlike honour of England on the issue of the coming day, the soldiers of Henry spent the night in repose, in making their wills and confessions, and preparing for battle with that gravity, order, and decorum which have ever been characteristic of British troops. The king himself took but little repose. He visited the different quarters of the army, and, during a brief season of moonlight sent certain captains of skill to examine the ground; and, to keep the hearts of the men cheerful, he ordered the trumpets, drums, and fifes to play at intervals during the night; but history fails to record the airs by which he sought to recall the memory of their homes, or the deeds of other days. So the night passed away; the French watch-fires died out, and the dawn stole on - the dawn of that great Feast of St. Crispin, the 25th of October, 1415. After solemn prayer, he formed his army in three great divisions, with two wings.

The archers, on whom he rested his principal hope, he posted in front of the men-at-arms. "Their well-earned reputation in former battles," says Lingard, tersely, "and their savage appearance on this day, struck terror into their enemies. Many had stripped themselves naked; the others had bared their arms and breasts, that they might exercise their limbs with more ease and execution. Besides his bow and arrows, battle-axe and sword, each bore a large, strong stake on his shoulder, which he was instructed to fix obliquely before him in the ground, and thus oppose a rampart to the charge of the French cavalry."

As Henry in the morning rode from division to division, and from banner to banner, mounted on a little grey palfrey at first, cheering and exhorting his troops, he chanced to hear a gentleman express a wish to a friend "that some of the good knights who were idle in England might by a miracle be transported to the field of battle."

"No," exclaimed King Henry, "I would not have a single man more. If God gives us the victory, it will be plain that we owe it to His goodness. If He do not, the fewer we are will be the less loss to England. But fight with your usual courage, and God and the justice of our cause shall protect us." A similar burst of courage was exhibited by a Welsh captain named David Gam, who, on being sent to reconnoitre the enemy, reported that "there were enough to be killed, enough to be taken, and enough to run away."

The French order of battle resembled the English, save that in some parts where the latter were but four files deep the former were thirty.

The Constable of France, Charles d'Albret, Comte de Dreux, led the first line; the Dukes of Bar and D'Alençon led the second; the Lords of Marie and Falconberg led the third. The distance between the two armies at first was about a quarter of a mile, and the ground between them was wet and marshy with the rain of the past night.

With the French army were 500 heavily-mailed men-at-arms, and a body, of crossbow-men, sent by John of Nevers, the Duke of Burgundy. Thus .the disproportion between the armies was enormous; indeed, so small was the force of the English, that in opposing the three lines of the enemy Henry had literally three battles to fight.

Before the action began Henry was surprised to see three French knights ride boldly across to the English lines, desiring to speak with him. One of them, Jacques, the Baron de Helly, Maréchal of France, had been a prisoner of war in England, where he was accused of having broken his parole; and he now took this opportunity of denying the charge, and offering to meet in single combat, and in front of both armies, any man who should dare to repeat it.

"This is not a time for single combats," replied the king. "Go tell your countrymen to prepare for battle before night; and doubt not that for the violation of your word you shall a second time forfeit your liberty, if not your life."

"Sire," retorted Helly, "I shall receive no orders from you. Charles is our sovereign; him we obey, and for him we shall fight against you whenever we think proper."

"Away, then; and take care I am not before you," cried Henry, stepping forward. "Banners, advance!"

Then Sir Thomas Erpingham threw his warder in the air, and the lines knelt while the men kissed - some say bit - the earth; and at the distance of twenty paces from the French the English ranks halted and raised a loud cheer.

Henry could only form two lines. Edward, Duke of Kent, led the first, aided by the Lords Beaumont and Willoughby and Sir John Cornwall, afterwards Baron Fanhope. Henry in person led the second, mounted on a white horse; near him floated the standard of England, and he was assisted by his brother, Humphrey, Duke of Gloucester; Mowbray, the Earl Marshal;

and the Earls' of Oxford and Suffolk. The men who were armed with spears, bills, and halberds closed the rear, under Thomas, Earl of Dorset, afterwards Duke of Exeter.

Prior to all this, and while the morning was dusk, the king had secretly detached a body of 400 lances, who concealed themselves in a wood on the enemy's left, while 200 archers were posted in a low meadow and hidden by bushes on their right. Aware that the enemy far exceeded him in cavalry, and that his infantry, the chief strength of his army, would probably be broken by the first charge, he had commanded some archers who were in the van to plant their stakes in front; but as the French did not advance, on the signal being made as described by Erpingham, the king cried, "Let us break through them, in the name of the Holy Trinity! "On this, the archers in front, under the Duke of York, began to pour their volleys upon the French; and being all chosen men, of great strength and dexterity, they did terrible execution, all the more so that the array of the enemy was so close or dense - being thirty files deep - that men could scarcely move. Spurring on their horses, and shouting their war-cries, the French men-at-arms came thundering on, with flashing lance and sword, to cut to pieces the archers; but the latter retreated quickly to the rear of their stakes, "a wonderful discipline, in which the king had exercised them himself for some days." Floundering amid the wet clayey soil, the mailed cavalry came on, only to recoil from the pointed stakes and that withering shower of arrows; while at the same moment the archers among the bushes on their flank now rose suddenly and opened upon them. The wounded men and horses discomposed the ranks; the narrow ground in which they were compelled to act hindered them from recovering order, and over all the French front began to reign confusion and dismay. Many of their horses sank to their knees in the mud.

As they began to recoil, the archers slung their bows, and

rushed among them with hatchets and halberds, swords and mallets, and all were now engaged in what the battles of those days always became - a wild and mingled mass of all arms, fighting men and horses. Henry, who had now dismounted and fought on foot, conspicuous alike by his valour, his glittering armour, and golden crown, in attempting to pierce the second line of French, under the Duke d'Alençon, was exposed to no ordinary danger. The Duke of Gloucester was beaten to the ground by the battle-axe of the Duke d'Alençon, but Henry drove back all about him, and saved his kinsman. Animated by rage and despair, the French prince now turned his weapon on Henry, and clove the gold crown on his helmet. Henry struck him to the ground, slew two of his attendants, and would have slain him, had not he called out -

"Hold, I yield; I am Alençon!"

On this the King of England held forth his hand, but the duke was instantly killed. Eighteen French knights had registered a solemn vow to slay the former, and some of these who fought their way to where they saw the royal standard flying actually

Henry and Alençon at Agincourt.

180

beat Henry down upon his knees - the chief of these were Brunelet de Massinguehem, and Ganio de Bornenville - but in a few minutes all of them perished to a man. "The French fell in heaps," says a writer, "some of these frightful piles reaching to the height of a man, from the top or the sides of which the two parties alternately fought, as if these mounds of carnage had been common ramparts." It was a miracle that Henry escaped, as he was a mark for the weapon of every Frenchman who could reach him. The death of Alençon so utterly discouraged the troops that, despite all the exertions of the Constable d'Albret, they began to take flight.

Their third line, being still fresh and in good order, might certainly have restored for France the failing fortune of the day; but their hearts were already sinking, and when they saw the 400 English lances advancing at a rapid trot from the wood upon their left flank, they gave way, and, without striking a blow, left to the mercy of an almost victorious enemy the broken troops of the second line, which it was their duty to cover and support. The conflict still continued, for now the English had nothing more to do than kill or capture as they pleased.

King Henry, perceiving that the troops of the third line were hovering at a little distance, as if preparing to return, sent to them a herald with a message to leave the field instantly or they should receive no quarter. This menace succeeded almost beyond his expectation, as they instantly retired, and the battle was won; but still the slaughter was not over. Word was suddenly brought to Henry that the routed enemy was now in his rear. Astonished by an incident so unexpected, he hurried to the summit of an eminence that lay between the field and his camp at Maisoncelles, and saw that the greatest disorder prevailed there. His baggage-guard was dispersed, and seeking flight from some unknown assailants. Supposing the battle was about to be renewed, he ordered the instant destruction of all the prisoners save those of rank; and a new and dreadful slaughter of the defenceless and unarmed continued till 14,000 were slain, before he discovered his mistake and stopped it. The broil in the camp was occasioned by a band of 600 fugitives, led by Robert de Bournonville, Isambart d'Agincourt, and others; who having left the battle "betimes," and knowing that Henry's camp was but slenderly protected, betook them to the work of pillaging it, till attacked and put to flight.

In this battle, so memorable alike to England and to France, the French lost the Constable d'Albret, the Dukes of Alençon and Brabant, the Connt de Nevers, the Duke of Bar, the Counts of Vaudemont, Marie, Roussi, and Falconberg, more than a hundred of different ranks who had banners borne before them, 1,500 knights, and 7,000 soldiers. Of the English there were slain only the Duke of York, the young Earl of Suffolk, and, if we are to believe certain English historians, four knights, one squire, and twenty-four soldiers. De Mezeray reckons the loss at 1,600 men, and Monstrelet at one hundred more than that number. The most eminent among the prisoners were the Dukes of Orleans and Bourbon, the Marshal Boucicault, and the-Counts of Vendome and Richemont. Orleans was found wounded, under a heap of dead, by the archers when plundering on the field; and perceiving some signs of life in him, they carried him to King Henry, who ordered him to be treated with all care and courtesy. He was author of some of the earliest poetical valentines known, and some written by him when in the Tower of London are now preserved in the British Museum. The king now sent for Montjoy, a French herald, who came for permission to bury the dead, and said to him -

"To whom belongs this victory?"

"To you, sire," replied Montjoy.

"And what castle is that which we can perceive in the distance?"

"It is called the castle of Agincourt, sire."

"Then let this be called the battle of Agincourt," said Henry. He further added that the sins of France, and not his soldiers, had wrought her defeat, and ordered the hymn, *"Non nobis, Domine,"* to be chanted by the whole army. To John Wodehouse, of Kimberly, in Norfolk, for bravery in this field, he granted an augmentation of honour to his coat-of-arms - viz., on the chevron, *gouttes de sang* (drops of blood), with the motto, *"Frappez fort."*

That shattered host could now achieve no more. Henry at once marched to Calais with his prisoners, and thence proceeded to Dover, where the people, in their joy to welcome a monarch so gallant and heroic, rushed into the water to receive and to bear him ashore. On the 23rd of November, just a month after the battle, and while the hearts of the people were brimming over with enthusiam, amid shouting crowds and waving banners, he made his triumphal entry into London. At Blackheath he was received by the mayor and aldermen, arrayed in orient grained scarlet, "and 400 commoners, in beautiful murrey, all with rich collars and chains, and on horseback." At St. Thomas à Watering he was met by all the clergy in solemn procession, with sumptuous vestments, crosses, and censers. The then quaint and narrow old streets were gaily decorated. A giant stood on the central tower of London Bridge; and a St. George, armed on all points, was placed at the gate next the city. The tower of the conduit on Cornhill was decked with scarlet cloth; the cross of Chepe was concealed by "a noble castle," from lence came forth "a chorus of virgins, with timbrel and dance, .as to another David coming from the slaughter of Goliath; and their song of congratulation was, 'Welcome, Henry the Fifte, king of England and France!'" And amid all this pageantry the king passed to his devotions in old St. Paul's: and so modest was he in his nature, it he would not permit his bruised and battered helmet to be exhibited, as a trophy of his valour, to the people; but after his death it was hung over his tomb in Westminster Abbey. There, to, were placed the shield and war-saddle he used on that terrible Feast of St. Crispin, at Agincourt, which put all France in mourning. Subsequent to that event there ensued some fighting by sea. To retake Harfleur, in which Henry had left a garrison under the Earl of Dorset, e French besieged it on the land side, under the new Constable d'Armagnac; while a squadron, under the Vice-Admiral Narbonne, with a fleet of Castilian and Genoese ships, which had attacked Portsmouth, Southampton, and the Isle of Wight, blocked it up by sea. Dorset made a brave defence, but he had only some 1,500 men, and being reduced to the direst extremity, he was on the point of capitulating, when a fleet of 400 sail, under the Duke of Bedford, having on board 20,000 English, was seen steering for the mouth of the Seine. Beford had with him the Earl Marshal, and the Earls of Oxford, Huntingdon, Warwick, Arundel, Salisbury, and Devonshire. Perceiving that it was impossible to succour the little garrison without first breaking rough the blockade formed by the combined fleets of the Constable, of John II of Castile (then an infant), and of the Genoese, whose ruler was Thomas Fregosso, an elective duke, he instantly made the signal for battle, and, being to windward, bore down upon them, grappled, and engaged. Long, bloody, and furious was the engagement; but the three allies were totally defeated, and 500 sail (among which were five Genoese carracks, ships from their size then supposed to be impregnable) were taken or sunk, with all on board. And as nothing then prevented the Duke of Bedford from throwing succour into Harfleur, the Constable raised the siege and retired. This signal sea-fight is said to have occurred about the end of July.

Henry V was undoubtedly the great restorer of the English navy, and during his brilliant career in France his attention was constantly directed to guarding the coast, and the erection of fortifications at Portsmouth and other places; and when, on the renewal of the war, in 1417, he made preparations for again returning to the Continent, when he embarked his army of 25,500 men at Dover his fleet consisted of 1,500 ships. Two of these vessels had sails of purple, adorned with the arms of England and France. One was named "the King's Chamber," the other "the King's Hall" - as a kind of proof that he affected to keep his Court at sea, and considered his ships royal, like his palace. In this force he had no less than 16,000 men-at-arms; and for the first time we hear of a long train of artillery," and other warlike engines, meaning those of the past ages. The shields of the knights on board the ships of those days were all fixed round the gunwale, as a kind of ornament and additional bulwark in battle.

BAUJÉ, 1421 - CREVANT, 1423 - VERNEUIL, 1424

BAUJÉ

WHEN HENRY re-landed in France, that country is rent by civil dissensions; and slowly but surely extended his conquests, until the fall of Rouen, after a siege of six months, laid all Normandy at his feet, while his path to the throne of France was opened by an unforeseen circumstance. The foul murder of the Duke of Burgundy threw all that Prince's faction, thirsting for vengeance, on the side of Henry. He was thus enabled to dictate the famous Treaty of Troyes, by which the crown of France was transferred to the House of Lancaster. How true seemed his reply to the Pope's legate, who urged peace shortly before this: - "Do you not see that God has led me hither as by the hand? France has no sovereign; I have just pretensions to that kingdom, and no one now thinks of resisting me. Can I have a more sensible proof that the Being who disposes of empires has determined to put the crown of France on my head?" The three leading conditions of the treaty were, that Henry would receive in marriage the French Princess Catherine; that he should be Regent of France during the life of the imbecile Charles VI; and that he should succeed to the French throne on that prince's death, an event easily brought about in those days. But a short visit to England with his bride was suddenly clouded by disastrous tidings, which quickly recalled him to France. Reinforced by a large body of Scots, under the Earl of Buchan, the Dauphin had routed the English at Baujé, and slain the Duke of Clarence, Henry's brother; and these events came about in the following manner.

Robert III, King of Scotland, fearing the power of his brother, resolved to send his son, Prince James, to France; but the vessel in which he embarked, being driven in a storm on the English coast, he was somewhat treacherously detained by Henry, who eventually gave the young prince a good education, which, however, failed to enable him to tame the fierce nobles and chiefs of his native kingdom. On these tidings coming to the castle of Rothesay, the old king died of grief. Years of a regency ensued in Scotland, and the young king was left unransomed in the hands of Henry. One of the secret springs of action in this affair has been fully explained by Tytler, in his historical remarks on the supposed death of Richard II, who was then believed to have escaped into Scotland, where he was fostered and protected by the Regent Albany, as a bugbear to Henry and his family. In the year 1419, when Albany was succeeded in the regency by his son, Murdoch, and while a war between England and Scotland was raging on the borders, the Due de Vendôme arrived as ambassador from Charles, the Dauphin of France, craving assistance against King Henry, and the request was not made in vain. The Scots, we are told, had beheld with natural alarm and jealousy the signal success of the English arms in France. If her ancient ally fell in the contest, it was just possible that Scotland might be humbled too; hence it was resolved to send succour: and it is somewhat remarkable that the first signal defeat sustained by the English on the soil of France came from the hands of their fellow-islanders.

Under Sir John Stuart, Earl of Buchan, youngest son of Robert, Duke of Albany, it was resolved to send an auxiliary force to France, in shipping that was to be provided by that country, and by Don Juan, King of Castile, and Alphonso the Infant of Arragon, with whom the Scots were in alliance. The two last-named princes promised a fleet of forty sail.

Henry, who was at home with his young French queen, on

hearing of these preparations, had ordered his brother, Bedford, the Regent of France, to leave no means untried for intercepting Buchan and his Scots upon the sea; but the order came too late, and in the summer of 1420, the earl, who had embarked with a force stated by Balfour at 10,000, by another at 7,000 men, was safely landed by the carracks of Castile and Arragon at Rochelle, whence they marched at once to the aid of the Dauphin, who was then about to attempt the reduction of Languedoc, and who by a courier informed the earl that he had been deceived by the pretended reconciliation at Pouilly le Fort with the new Duke of Burgundy.

Among the Scottish leaders who came with Buchan, were Sir John Stewart of Darnley (constable of the troops), who was slain at the siege of Orleans, in 1429; Archibald Douglas, Earl of Wigton, afterwards Lord of Longueville and Marshal of France; Sir Henry Cunningham of Kilmaurs; Sir Robert Houston; Sir Hew Kennedy; Sir Alexander Buchanan, of that ilk, and Sir John Swinton, of that ilk, both slain at Verneuil; Sir John Carmichael; Sir William Crawford, killed at the siege of Clavell; Sir Robert Maxwell, of Calderwood, who died of his wounds at Chinon; and others, like them, all well-trained in the ceaseless warfare of those stormy times. This expedition brings us to the earliest authentic record of an important feature in British history, the influence of the Scots in France; and in the War Office "Records of the First Regiment of Foot," which now represents in an unbroken line the Scots of Lord Buchan, we find the following paragraph: - "It is recorded in history that so early as the year 882, Charles III of France had twenty-four armed Scots, in whose fidelity and valour he reposed confidence, to attend his person as a guard. When Henry V, after having gained the memorable victory at Agincourt, was acknowledged as heir to the French throne by Charles VI, the Scots guard appear to have quitted the Court and taken part with the. Dauphin, afterwards Charles VII, in his resistance to the new arrangement, which deprived him of the succession to the crown. At that time 7,000 men were sent from Scotland, under the Earl of Buchan, to assist the Dauphin; and these auxiliaries having evinced signal gallantry on several occasions, especially at the battle of Baujé", &c., Charles selected from among them 100 men-at-arms and 100 archers for the protection of the royal person, subsequently, designated the 'Gendarmes Ecossaises.' The Scots continued with the French army, and signalised themselves at the capture of Avranches, in Normandy, in 1422; and at the battle of Crevant, in 1423. An additional force of 5,000 men was sent from Scotland in 1424; and the Scots gave proof of personal bravery at the battle of Vemeuil, and in the attack on the English convoy under Sir John Fastolfe, in 1429; and after these repeated instances if gallantry, Charles VII selected a number of Scots Gentlemen of quality and approved valour, whom e constituted a guard, and to which he gave precedence over all the other troops in France, and this guard was designated 'Le Garde du Corps Ecossaises.'"

To Buchan and his Scots were first assigned the town and castle of Chatillon, in Touraine. Of their constitution some information is given us by the ales for war drawn up by the late King Robert III, for the regulation of the Scottish and French forces. Pillage was forbidden, under pain of death. Any soldier killing another was to be instantly executed; any soldier striking a gentleman was to lose his and or his ears; any gentleman defying another 'as to be put under arrest. If knights rioted, they were to be deprived of their horses and armour; and whoever unhorsed an Englishman was to have half his ransom." Blows were soon exchanged between them and the English and Burgundians. Sir Robert Maxwell was mortally wounded, and expired at Chinon, bequeathing by will his coat of mail to is brother John, "and ten pounds to his little footage." Their success in France so enraged King Henry, that he brought over with him in his next expedition the captive King of Scotland, in whose name he ordered Buchan and his forces to abstain from all acts of hostility. But to this the earl relied, "that so long as his sovereign was a captive, and under the control of others, he did not feel himself bound to obey him." This so enraged Henry that when he captured Meaux he slaughtered thirty Scotsmen whom he found there in cold blood, on the plea "that they bore anus against their own king."

From the Chronicle of Monstrelet, we learn that the Duke of Clarence, who had been appointed Governor of Normandy, after being joined by Sir Thomas Beaufort and two Portuguese captains of free Lances, marched on Easter-eve towards Anjou, to attack the Scots and Dauphinois, who were led by Lord Buchan, the Lord de la Fayette, who was Seneschal of the Bourbonnois, and the Vicomte de Tarbonne, who so lately fought against the Duke of Bedford at Harfleur. Halting on his march to dine, he had barely sat down to table when he was informed by Andrea Fregosa, an Italian deserter, that the forces of the Earl of Buchan were encamped twenty two miles eastward of Angers, at the small town of Baujé. On this the gallant Clarence prang from table, and exclaimed, "Let us attack them they are ours! But let none follow me save the men-at-arms."

He immediately set forth with all his knights and cavalry; "beside his other gallant furniture and rich armour," wearing round his helmet a royal coronet set with many jewels. The Earl of Salisbury was to follow at all speed, with 4,000 infantry and archers. The Scots and the Dauphinois were, we have said, at Baujé, situated on the Couanon river, which was there crossed by an ancient bridge, and the battle which ensued there resembles in some of the features the greater one fought at Stirling by Wallace and the Earl of Surrey a hundred and twenty years before. The Couanon was both deep and rapid, and its narrow bridge was the only means by which these foes could approach each other. Under Sir John Stewart, of Darnley, and the Sieur de la Fontaine, Buchau had sent forward a reconnoitring party, who saw in time the glittering lances of Clarence advancing, and fell back duly to warn the camp, where the immediate cry was "To arms!" and Buchan drew up his forces in order of battle in front of the town, on the 22nd of March, 1421. Clarence, we are told, was inspired by hot anger on finding the passage of the river was to be disputed by the Scots; and he might have remembered at such a time the old English proverb, which Shakespeare afterwards introduced in his "Henry V" -

"There's a saying very old and true -
If that you will France win,
Then with Scotland first begin.'"

Salisbury had orders to cross the Couanon by a ford, and turn the flank of the Scots if he could; while Clarence came on direct for the bridge with a glittering array of men-at-arms, all clad in magnificent armour.

To prevent its passage being forced, its defence was entrusted to Sir Robert Stewart, of Railston, with only thirty archers; and just as the skirmish began, Sir Hew Kennedy, son of the Knight of Dunure, who was quartered in a church close by, rushed forth at the head of 100 Scots, who, in their hurry, had their armour only half-buckled; but who, by a flanking shower of arrows, drove the English back for a space. The Earl of Buchan now dashed forward, at the head of 200 chosen knights, and in the high narrow passage of the ancient bridge there ensued a dreadful, and to Clarence most fatal, combat. Inspired by the mutual hate and rancour that more than a hundred years of war engendered between them, the English and Scots, now meeting on French soil, fought with the fury of madmen. The former, says Buchanan, "took in it great disdain that they should be

191

attacked by such an implacable enemy, not only at home, but beyond the seas; so they fought stoutly, but none more so than Clarence himself, who was well known by his armour."

On the other hand, Buchan, a powerful man, in the forty-second year of his age, fought with all the courage and resolution of his race; but Clarence, being distinguished by his fatal coronet, was the mark of every weapon. In the close mêlée of mounted men upon the bridge, he was almost instantly assailed by Sir John Carmichael, ancestor of the future Earls of Hyndford, who, with helmet closed and lance in rest, spurred upon him with such fury that the tough ash shaft was broken to shivers upon the corselet of the prince, who at the same moment was wounded in the face by Sir John Swinton; then, just as he was falling from his high war-saddle, the Earl of Buchan dashed out his brains by one blow with an iron mace - Gods-croft calls it "a steell hammer" - to which he had resorted after running him through the body with his lance. The fall of so gallant a prince filled the English knights and men-at-arms with greater fury, and they pressed in crowds upon the bridge to avenge him; in their haste and confusion, jostling and impeding each other in such a fashion that they were driven back, put to flight, and cut to pieces by the Scots, who continued the pursuit of the fugitives till night came on. Monstrelet has it that 3,000 English fell; Walter Bower says 1,700, while the French lost twelve, and the Scots only two, a disparity utterly incredible, as we find in the Chronicle of the former that the Dauphinois lost 1,100 men, among whom were Sir John Yvorin, Garin des Fontaines, and the good knight, Sir Charles le Bouteiller.

Among the English there fell Gilbert de Umphreville, titular Earl of Angus, in Scotland; the Lord de Roos, of Hamlake; the Lord of Tancarville; and Sir John Grey, of Heton. Two hundred, with their horses and armour, fell into the hands of the Scots; among them were John, Earl of Somerset, whose sister, Jane

Beaufort, was afterwards Queen-Consort of Scotland, and Henry, Earl of Huntingdon, son of Richard II's half sister.

Buchan bestowed the dead body of Clarence on the Earl of Salisbury, and John, the bastard of Clarence. They bore it unmolested to Rouen, and thence to England, where it was interred at the feet of his father, in Canterbury Cathedral, as the duke had directed by a will written before the battle, but his coronet was retained by the Scots. Sir John Stuart, of Darnley, purchased it from one of his soldiers for 1,000 angels, and Sir Robert Houston afterwards lent him five times that sum upon it. Buchanan, on the authority of the lost "Book of Pluscardine," asserts that it was Sir Alexander Macauslan, a knight of the Lennox, who took the diadem from the helmet of Clarence. Sir John Carmichael, in memory of shivering his spear on the duke's breast, added to his arms a hand grasping a broken spear; though the honour of unhorsing him was claimed by Swinton and the Laird of Auchmar. To the shield of Sir Hew Kennedy the King of France added azure, three fleurs-de-lys or, in memory of his defence of the bridge, and these are till borne by all of the surname of Kennedy who are descended from him.

On the victor, Buchan, was now bestowed the word and office of Constable of France, of which Charles of Lorraine had been the last holder. He was the first stranger to whom such an honour had teen given, and it was followed by other gifts, such as castles and princely domains, stretching over all he territory between Chartres and Avranches.

The Earl of Buchan, after capturing the castle of he former place, laying siege to the old fortress of Uengon, and repulsing with the loss of 400 men Lord Salisbury, who attempted its relief, was compiled to return to Scotland, in consequence of the feuds which had broken out there. He left Stewart if Darnley commander, or, as he was named, "Constable of the Scots in France."

CREVANT

Henry V was now master of all northern France to the banks of the Loire. Save at Baujé, no leaf had fallen from the laurels he had won at Agincourt; but just as he had almost won the summit of his ambition he died, and, surviving him by only two months, Charles VI of France also passed way on the 21st October, 1422. John of Bedford, le persecutor of Joan of Arc, immediately ordered is young nephew, Henry VI, to be proclaimed King of France; whilst the Dauphin, now Charles II, to whom the Scots adhered, was called in mockery by the English and Burgundians, "King of Bourges," as these two powers held all the provinces that lay between the Loire and the Scheldt.

All the bravest captains in France and all the princes of the royal blood adhered to Charles; and we are told by Monstrelet that early in July, 1423, "he ordered a large body of forces to cross the Loire, and besiege the town of Crevant. The chief of his expedition was," he adds, "the Constable of Scotland," a mistake of the chronicler, for Stewart of Darnley was simply Constable of the Scots, who had soon reason to regret the absence of their former leader, as Stewart, though brave, was destitute of military skill. Rapin states that the troops which crossed the Loire were commanded by the Maréchal de Severac; but he only led the French. Crevant, which they besieged, lies six miles southeast of Auxerre, and the river Yonne was between them and the united English and Burgundians, at whose approach, 15,000 strong, Stewart drew up his forces in order of battle on the slope of a hill. The blockaded town was in his rear; before him rolled the river, which was crossed there by a stone bridge.

At Dijon the Duchess of Burgundy had urged that, at all hazards, Crevant should be saved from the Scots and French; whereupon the Lord de Toulongeon, Maréchal of Burgundy, united his forces to those of the Earls of Salisbury and Suffolk, with whom came Lord Willoughby, one of the heroes of Agincourt, and many more brave knights. The armour of the French man-at-arms of this period differed a little from that used by his English rival. Back and breast-plates were worn. To these were attached "a system of articulated lames, or narrow plates, in their contour adapted to cover the figure, and so arranged that each one should slightly overlap the one below it; thus was formed a species of kilt of armour. Over the flanks, on each side of the figure, to the faudes or taces was appended a small shield, or garde-faude, which would cover the front of the thigh, and, being secured by only buckles and straps, would allow free movement to the limb. These plates appear in every variety of form - square, hexagonal, lozenge-shaped, serrated, &c. In front and also behind, the haubergeon was shown uncovered." "Such," says Boutell, "was the armour worn by the brothers of Charles VI, the Sires des Fleurs de Lis, when they went to war. Such also was the armour of the famous Duke of Burgundy, John the Fearless, who caused the Duke of Orleans to be assassinated; and the same armour was worn by the nobles of Armagnac and of Burgundy who, in the fifteenth century, desolated France with such ferocious rapacity." Gauntlets of steel were then recent inventions in France, where previously a strong leather glove had been the sole protection for the hand of the soldier.

The troops of Lord Salisbury suffered much on their march, by the weight of their armour and the extreme heat of the sun, especially the gendarmerie, many of whom marched on foot, leading by the bridle their horses, that the latter might be more fresh for battle. As they drew near Crevant, 120 English and Burgundian horse, with the same number of archers, were sent forward as a reconnoitring party. Each archer had a pointed stake, to plant in the earth if necessary, to keep off cavalry. In Auxerre the English and Burgundians heard mass celebrated;

"drank a cup in much brother-like affection; and departed to fall upon the Scots and French, who had been under arms all night, and towards whom they advanced in handsome array, at ten o'clock on the morning of Saturday."

Sir John Stewart had under his orders 3,000 Scots, with some French under Aumaury, the Maréchal de Severac, the Lord of Estissac, and the Comte de Ventadour. With their troops in solid array, and with all their armour shining in the morning sun, he and those leaders sat quietly in their saddles, while the adverse forces surveyed each other for three hours; after which "they tamely permitted the English and their allies to defile across the bridge of the Yonne, and then to arrange their squares of foot and squadrons of men-at-arms, when they ought to have occupied the *tête-du-pont* with cannon and crossbow-men, or have attacked them when half their strength was over. The most simple lessons of military art and tactics were forgotten by these leaders, and most disastrous was the result."

Then, without striking a blow, nearly the whole of the French, the confidence of whose soldiery had been destroyed at Agincourt, fell back, under the Seigneur de Severac, and left the field to the Scots, who stood firm. A writer asserts that in most of the encounters at this time "the French generally ran away, and left the Scots to fight for them."

Overlapped and overwhelmed by the superior strength of the English and Burgundians, who assailed them in front and on both flanks, while a sortie from Crevant came upon their rear, the unlucky Scots fell into disorder. Stewart fought desperately to repair his first error, but lost an eye in the conflict, by a sword-thrust through the ventaille of his helmet; and becoming thereby blinded with blood, he surrendered himself to a Burgundian noble, Claude de Beauvoir, of Castellux.

"Le Connestable d'Escosse," according to "Mémoires Historiques," Vol. VII, "descendit à pied, et avec lui plusieurs vaillans Français et Escossais, croyons que Severac et les autres deusent ainsi faire; ou au moins frapper à cheval sur les ennemies: il y fut fort combatu, et finalement les Français et Escossais furent defaits et y en eut plusiers de tuez et pris, jusques au nombere de deux à trois mille, qui fut un grand dommage pour les Roy de France." Following up the mistake of Monstrelet, it is stated by De Mezeray, that "the Constable de Bouchain and the Maréchal de Severac were beaten, and 1,000 of their most valiant soldiers lay dead upon the plain, and almost as many were led away prisoners, among whom were the Constable and the Count de Ventadour."

The latter, who had also lost an eye, surrendered to the Lord of Gamaches; and John Poton, Lord of Xaintrailles, was also taken.

Of the Scots, 1,200 were killed, and among them are enumerated by Monstrelet a nephew of the Earl of Buchan, Sir William Hamilton, and his son, Sir Thomas Swinton, and "John Pillot, a Scots captain, and bastard to the king." Sir William Crawford and 400 were taken prisoners. Among the English who fell were Sir Gilbert Halselle, Sir John Grey, Sir William Hall, and Richard Ap Murdoc. The English and Burgundians offered up solemn thanks in the churches of Crevant for this victory.

Sir John Stewart was exchanged for the Lord Pole; and after being made Lord of Aubigny, Concressault, and Evereux, with the right of quartering the arms of France with his own, he was slain in his old age at the siege of Orleans.

VERNEUIL

Shortly after the battle of Crevant, Réné of Chartres, who was Chancellor of France, and Juvenal des Ursins, Archbishop of Rheims, the historian of the reign of Charles VI, were sent to

Scotland for mere auxiliaries, and another small force took service under the Constable Buchan for that purpose. The Earl of Douglas, he who lost an eye at Homildon, who fought at Shrewsbury, and defended Edinburgh Castle with such success against King Henry, in 1409 - on being created Duke of Touraine and Maréchal of France, joined him with a body of horse and foot. Holinshed states the number of this new force at 10,000 men, but there is reason to suppose they were far fewer. Their leaders were Adam Douglas, afterwards Governor of Tours; Bernard Lindesay, of the house of Glenesk; the Laird of Smailholm, who was armour-bearer to Earl Douglas; two other Douglases, who were the ancestors of the lines of Lochleven and Queensberry; and a very aged border warrior, Sir Alexander Home, of that ilk.

Landing at Rochelle in the spring of 1424, they joined the other Scottish troops, then in Poitou, under Charles VII. At this time the Duke of Bedford had laid siege to Ivri-la-Bataille, a Norman town, which a brave knight, named Girault de la Palliere, was defending, but had agreed to surrender if not succoured by a certain day; so Charles resolved to hasten to its relief. With difficulty he collected 18,000 men, one-half of whom were Scots, "under the Earls of Douglas, Buchan, and Murray," according to Monstrelet. The French were under De Ventadour, De Tonnere, and the Viscount of Narbonne; while Buchan, in right of his office as Constable of France, commanded the whole, though Monstrelet, in his account of the battle that ensued, always gives the preference to the Duke of Alençon.

The Regent Bedford, with 18,000 men-at-arms and 8,000 archers, with the Lords Salisbury, Suffolk, and Willoughby, having reinforced those troops which blockaded Ivry, the relieving force came too late, or just in time to see St. George's cross waving on the walls, with an English garrison in possession, under a knight of Wales. On this Buchan and Alençon marched several miles further to Verneuil, on the Arve. The old walls by which it was then surrounded still exist, and also the tower into which its English garrison retired on their approach. To this place Bedford now hastened with all his available troops, while about the exact number of the Constable's force no two authors agree. Hall says he had 5,000 Scots and 15,000 French; Père Daniel has it only 14,000 men, one-half of whom were Scots. However, the combined force was marched to Verneuil by the Earl of Buchan as leader, "who then," says Rapin, "was pleased to resign that honour to the Earl of Douglas, his father-in-law, to whom the king sent for that purpose (i.e., to command) a patent constituting him lieutenant-general of the whole kingdom, otherwise the Constable could not have acted under his orders."

On both sides the forces were apparently pretty equal; and when within a mile of Verneuil the Duke of Bedford sent a herald and trumpeter to "Le Maréchal Comte de Du Glas," as the French styled the earl, to say that "he would come and

La Rochelle.

dine with him;" to which Douglas, who had long been wont to ridicule the English regent as "John with the Leaden Sword," sent for answer that "he was welcome, as the cloth was ready laid."

Bedford was resolved to wait an attack; and, knowing the fiery nature of those allies he had come to oppose, he judiciously selected a piece of ground suitable alike for fighting or camping. It was flanked by a hill whereon he posted 2,000 archers, and along his front he planted a row of those pointed stakes introduced at Agincourt for the repelling of cavalry.

Douglas drew up his troops in order of battle before the walls of Verneuil. To the Constable Buchan, with the Scots, he assigned the centre; the command of the wings he gave to the Viscount of Narbonne, and Gilbert, the Maréchal de la Fayette. Each wing he covered by 1,000 mounted men-at-arms, completely mailed, with lance, battle-axe, and barbed horses. Those on the right flank were led by the Lords of Thionville and Estissac, and two Marshals of France, viz., the Seigneur de Xaintrailles, and Philippe de Culant, Seigneur de Jaloignes. Those On the left flank were led by the Lords Laquin de Rue and Valpergue. In his ranks were some raw peasantry, but he had a body of 900 Lombard crossbow-men, who had been sent by the Duke of Milan, and who were all on horseback and in armour.

Douglas, after reconnoitering the English position, urged before a Council of War "that as the Duke of Bedford, instead of advancing, evidently intended to fight with advantage on strong and intrenched ground chosen by himself, no battle should be risked."

On this many of the French leaders, but chiefly the Viscount de Narbonne, who was jealous of Douglas, declared that if a battle were avoided the honour of France would suffer. Then the viscount - a fierce soldier, who was among the slayers of the

Duke of Burgundy - ordering his banner to be displayed, and, in defiance of all orders and advice, began to march with his own followers towards the enemy. Hall and Père Daniel record that "Douglas was infuriated by this disobedience, but that neither he nor the Constable could avert the purpose of those rash French lords. At home in Scotland they would have left them to their fate, or might perhaps have ended the matter more readily by killing their leader on the spot. But Douglas was in a foreign land, and afraid that his honour might suffer if the field was lost by only half his troops being engaged; and so, compelled by this fear, he issued orders for the whole to advance up the hill, and attack the position of the English."

It was at three o'clock in the afternoon of the 16th of August, 1424, that this somewhat important battle began - a battle all accounts of which are confused, but on the issue of which the fate of Charles VII and of France seemed to depend; for Bedford had now reduced every town and castle beyond the Loire.

The mass of Douglas's army was on foot; and his Lombard crossbow-men had special orders to attack the English archers, two bodies of which protected Bedford's wings, each, as we have said, with a pointed stake before him, planted at an angle of forty-five degrees. In rear of the English men-at-arms were the grooms and pages, with such horses as were unfit for battle, with their collars and tails tied together, so that they could not, if surprised, be carried off with ease. Over these was a guard composed of 2,000 archers.

Monstrelet records that "the English as usual set up a great shout," which alarmed the French very much. At the time when the centre column of Scots, under Buchan, came to blows with the English, the Lombard crossbow-men had galloped round to their rear, and there - after failing to make the slightest impression on the stake-protected flanks - they had fallen on the baggage-guard, and, after contriving to cut off a number of sumpter horses, deliberately fled. And now the Viscount of Narbonne, inspired by fresh anger and jealousy on finding that the Scots, half-breathless though they were from their up-hill march, had first encountered the enemy, according to some accounts maliciously withheld his division from supporting them in a proper manner, in that very conflict which his rashness had brought about.

Though the 2,000 mailed horse who covered the extreme flanks attacked the English archers, and, forcing a passage beyond the stakes, broke through the ranks and slew or trampled great numbers of them under hoof, their clothyard shafts from other points soon told with deadly effect on the Scots under Buchan, and the column of La Fayette. The centre, improperly supported, began to retire, though all the nobles and knights, forseeing the ruin and disaster that a defeat would ensure, fought with heroic courage, using their swords, maces, and battle-axes in the closest conflictions more than an hour: and during that time, choosing rather to die on the field than survive it with reproach, there fell the Constable Buchan; his father-in-law, the veteran Earl of Douglas; Hop-Pringle, of Smailholm; Sir Robert Stewart; Sir John Swinton, of that ilk; Sir Alexander Home, of that ilk; two Sir James Douglases; Sir Walter Lindesay; De Ventadour; the Viscount of Narbonne; the Lords Graville and Rambouillet; the Comte d'Aumale, and many gallant knights from Languedoc and Dauphine", with 5,000 men, "the greater part of whom were Scotsmen," says Enguerrand de Monstrelet, in his Chronicle. Many were wounded, and among them was found by the English, who remained masters of the field, the young Duke of Alençon half dead.

He states the English loss at 1,600; among these were two captains, named Dudley and Carleton. Holinshed, on the authority of Montjoy, the English King of Arms, who was present, gives the losses at 9,700 French and Scots, and that of the English at 2,100. Next day Bedford found in Verneuil the military chest, and all the baggage-of the French, Scots, and Italians. The latter, on being informed that Douglas and the Constable were victorious, had the hardihood to revisit the field, where they were unhorsed and shot down in the twilight by the English archers, who stripped the dead and wounded of their armour, and even of their clothing.

As the English marched into Verneuil, on the 17th of August, they met the body of Narbonne being borne forth for interment; and as his sword had been the first to pierce John the Undaunted, at the bridge of Monterreau, they quartered his remains and hung them on a gibbet.

The bodies of the Constable and of Douglas were found covered with wounds, and they were borne from the field with honour by the English, and were interred in one grave, in the cathedral church of St. Gratian, at Tours; and there and at Orleans, so lately as 1643, mass was offered up daily for the souls of the Scots who died in the cause of Charles VII.

The survivors of Verneuil he incorporated in his Garde du Corps Escossais.

ROVERAI, 1429

PRIOR TO the disastrous Wars of the Roses, England fought no great conflict either by land or sea, save one known in history by the curious title of the "Battle of the Herrings," in which Sir John Fastolfe, with whose name Shakespeare has made us so familiar under another spelling, figured conspicuously.

After the victory at Verneuil, where more men fell on both sides than in any battle since Agincourt, the power of Bedford in France grew weak; for the Duke of Gloucester, on his marriage with Jacqueline of Bavaria, claimed a part of the Netherlands as her inheritance; the Duke of Brabant, who also claimed to be her husband, opposed him, and was supported by the Duke of Burgundy, who thus became estranged from the English alliance. Subsidies came from London grudgingly, and then the Maid of Orleans came upon the scene. In the year before this, 1428, the Regent, contrary to his own wish, was compelled, we are told, by the Council to consent that the English army should cross the Loire and ravage those provinces which owned the sway of Charles, who, since the defeat to Verneuil, had been in ignoble retirement, where e lived with boon companions, contemplating only flight to Scotland or to Spain. As a preparatory step, the Regent besieged Orleans, which was so situated between the provinces commanded by England and those possessed by Charles, that it opened an easy entrance to either, and being wrongly fortified, was one of the most important aces in France. The eyes of all Europe were turned to this scene of action, and numberless deeds of courage and bravery were performed alike! the besiegers and besieged; but the blockade is enforced so strictly, and the general plan of tack was so vigorous, that

Charles of France gave over the city for lost, especially after the affair at Roverai which we are about to narrate. Cannon were extensively used in this siege, and by a shot from one of these, Thomas Montacute, the gallant Earl of Salisbury, fell. At the head of the English troops he had succeeded in capturing the tower on the bridge, and was looking over Orleans from one of the windows, when a cannon-shot carried away an eye and a cheek, one side of his face; and he expired a day or two after at Melun, leaving the command to the Earl of Suffolk.

This event, together with the duration of the siege, which had now lasted four months, confirmed the Regent Bedford in his first opinion, that the undertaking was a rash one. However, to neglect nothing that was in his power to further the end in view, as the season of Lent was at hand, he sent from Paris an immense supply of fish, chiefly salted herrings, together with a train of artillery, shot, powder, and other stores, in 500 carts, escorted by 1,700 men, under Sir John Fastolfe, one of the bravest and most skillful generals possessed by England at that time, and one whom Henry VI created Knight of the Garter. Under his orders were Sir Thomas Rampston and Sir Philip Hall, together with 1,000 followers, says Monstrelet, in addition to the troops - meaning, probably, wagoners and grooms.

King Charles having received notice of the very day on which the convoy was to leave Paris, resolved to cut it off, and dispatched Louis de Bourbon, the Count of Clermont, with 3,000 men, on the Orleans road for this purpose. With Clermont were the cuirassiers and archers of the Scottish Guard, under the Count d'Aubigny and John Stewart of Darnley (ancestor of the Dukes of Lennox), and the lances of the Count Dunois.

They came up with Fastolfe's convoy at Roverai, at seven in the morning of the 12th February, 1429. The glitter of armour and lances had warned Fastolfe of their approach; and making a kind of barricade of the wagons and carriages, he formed his men behind it. The French and Scottish men-at-arms alighted from their horses, and attacked this range entrenchment with sword and battle-axe, bile the yeomen behind it plied their bows. This movement was prematurely begun by the Scots, who were eager to avenge the day of Verneuil, and the Counts of Clermont and Dunois had placed me cannon in position, which they hoped would insure a victory. By lance, bill, and bow, the sailants were driven back, and the moment they gave way Fastolfe ordered some of the wagons to: drawn aside, and issuing forth, he charged them sword in hand. After a short but sharp conflict, the French and Scots were routed, and their cannon taken. Stewart of Darnley and one of his sons were slain. Monstrelet says the Count of Dunois was wounded, and that there fell six score of great lords and 500 men. This action was deemed of great importance in its time, as the convoy contained a vast quantity of provision necessary for the English during the season of Lent The bastard of Orleans, who had sallied out to assist Clermont in cutting it off, preserved sufficient presence of mind in the confusion of the rout to cape Fastolfe and to reach the city with 400 men. The successor of Darnley at the head of the Scottish Guard was a native of Dundee, named Robert Patullo, a soldier so famed for his success in many affairs in Guienne that he was called "The Little King of Gascony."

In the small affair of Roverai, the English proved, in greater fields, their vast superiority over the French. With a love and aptitude for manly exercises, the yeomanry of England were that the French were not - sturdy and muscular; moreover, they were cherished and respected by those lords and knights who led them in battle. "Nothing," says Froude, in his History, "proves more surely the mutual confidence which held together the Government and the people than the fact that all classes were armed." But very different was the state of the commonalty in France, who re then trampled on and despised by the nobles, as the latter arrogated to themselves alone the honour of bearing arms. Brantome has recorded that even in the fifteenth century the French infantry was composed of the most wretched class of the people; and that if any of these unfortunate men chanced to distinguish themselves in battle, they so excited the jealousy of their own gendarmerie, that they were sometimes charged by them and beaten down as if they were common enemies. "Thus," says Boutell, "while in one country a martial spirit was earnestly cherished, in the other it was rigorously repressed; and while the English archer had his natural manly qualities developed and matured, while he himself was highly esteemed and his services were suitably acknowledged, the French foot-soldier was conscious that for him to possess and exhibit any true military qualities was simply to imperil his own life."

Long before the dream of an English empire in France ended, in 1451, when Charles came in triumph from the South, and St. George's cross could be seen nowhere save on the citadel

The Battle of the Herrings.

of Calais, the use of cannon had become fully recognised as a necessary institution in battle and siege; but so defective were these pieces, that it was the arrow, the lance, and the sword that still decided all great conflicts. No man, either on horse or foot, as yet deemed it necessary to disencumber himself of any part of his defensive armour, because a single, and then unwieldy, machine had been invented, against which all armour was useless. The shield was going out of fashion; but additional plates screwed on certain parts of the armour replaced it. In fact, in Britain until the union of the crowns both cavalry and infantry carried nearly the same weight of panoply that had been worn in the days of Edward and Bruce; and it was not until the sixteenth century that, by the improvements in artillery, field-guns could be moved with requisite ease and expedition. The ancient cannon were without trunnions, and could neither be depressed nor elevated, as they lay on a species of slide. Richard II had no less than 400 such pieces at St. Malo in 1378. Some enormous bombardes, such as the "Great Lion," 3,000 pounds in weight, cast for James I of Scotland, in Flanders, in 1430 (Balf., Annales); Mons Meg, at Edinburgh; and two of the same calibre, nineteen inches, at St. Michael, in Normandy, were fashioned in the early part of the fifteenth century; but these were built of hoops and bars; and the artillerists of those days could not in their wildest dreams have imagined cannon such as we now manufacture at Woolwich, which will send a steel shot through fifteen inches of armour-plate, or carry a 600-pound ball from Woolwich into the city of London, a distance of seven miles.

Under Henry VI we find the first sign of an important change in warfare. The Italians conceived the use of a piece of ordnance small enough to be portable; hence the iron tube called a hand-cannon, fixed to a wooden stock, with a touch-hole on the top, and a pan to hold the powder. So early as 1446 one of these weapons, called then a "gonne," was used in England, as appears from a roll of purchases for the castle of Holy Island.

We now come to the battles of that time when a cloud, at first no bigger than a man's hand, began to darken round the throne of the House of Lancaster. Henry VI reigned, but visions of a crown began to rise in the mind of Richard, Duke of York, who sprang by his mother from the second son, and by his father from the fifth son of Edward III. The removal of a faithful minister from Henry's councils gave new colour to the hopes of York, and the cloud soon burst into the flame of a civil war. A son had been born to Henry VI, amid the rejoicings consequent to the suppression of Cade's insurrection; but the anger of the people had been excited by the bestowal of the royal favour on Somerset, whom they blamed for the loss of Normandy, and the failure of an attempt to recover Guienne; and at this time, so critical for the country, the king was seized with insanity. The reins of government were then committed to the Duke of York, with the title of Protector. Henry recovered, but York, having tasted the sweets of power, took up arms against him; and hence began the Wars of the Roses, so called from the badges of the rival armies, that of the House of York being a white, and that of the House of Lancaster being a red rose. The chief supporters of the daring and ambitious York were the Earl of Salisbury and his son, the Earl of Warwick. Essentially a war of the nobles, in which the mass of the people took little part, or which they looked on with indifference, it eventually shattered to its foundation the feudal system in England.

In this desolating strife were fought thirteen pitched battles, irrespective of skirmishes and the storming of castles; and of these battles, those that follow are the chief, and the best calculated to illustrate the mode of warfare and the rancorous; spirit of the times.

- C H A P T E R   X V I I -

BLORE HEATH, 1459 - ST. ALBANS; TOWTON, 1461 - BARNET, 1471

BLORE HEATH

THERE WERE two battles at St. Albans; the first was in 1455, when the Yorkists suddenly came upon the troops of the king. Both parties were almost entirely composed of gentlemen, and after a hand-to-hand combat in the steep old streets, the Royalists were beaten and the king made prisoner. After a pretended reconciliation, he was released. Again the war was renewed, and again the Yorkists were victorious, at Blore Heath, in the county of Stafford, and on the border of Shropshire; after a scuffle and some bloodshed in London, when Warwick had to fly, had renewed the hatred and suspicion of both parties.

The Duke of York had summoned his supporters to meet him at Kenilworth, where he and the Earl of Salisbury took measures to execute their projects against the king. They arranged that while the duke was levying an army in Wales, the earl should march at once on London, at the head of a force amounting to about 6,000 men, and openly demand satisfaction for the affront put upon his son. As these movements could not take place without the knowledge of the Queen Margaret of Anjou, James Tuchet, or Touchet, Lord Audley, was commissioned to raise troops in the quarter where his power and seigniory lay, to oppose Salisbury, whom, according to Hall, he had orders to bring in dead or alive. Moreover, he was to move against him with all speed. In a short time Audley was at the head of 10,000 men, and was able to march towards Lancashire, through which he supposed the earl must pass; but found that he was already as far as Shropshire, where Audley halted and encamped on Blore Heath, then an open waste or common, near a little stream, the Dove.

Salisbury, though his forces were but half the other's strength, had no thought of retreating or avoiding a battle, but there, on the 23rd September, 1459,01 the conflict which ensued, he supplied the defect in his numbers by stratagem; a refinement of which there occur few instances in the English civil wars, where headlong courage and strength of hand, rather than military tact or skill, were to be found.

Feigning a retreat, he retired in the night in such peculiar order that, when day broke, the loyalists could still perceive his troops, but only the rear of them. Audley, an ardent and gallant spirit (whose father, Sir John Touchet, had fallen in a sanguinary engagement with the Spaniards off Rochelle), now began to follow him with precipitation, but his vanguard had scarcely passed the brook, and become entangled among trees, roots, rocks, and stones, his high-spirited knights, all well mounted and clad in shining armour, with waving plumes, conceiving that they had nothing to do but overtake and cut down a flying enemy, than the Yorkists, who were in no disorder, and only waited or the troops of Audley to fall into the lure prepared or them, wheeled about, and closed in upon them in all sides, with bill and spear. When the conflict began, some only were across the stream and others were actually in the centre of it; yet the battle lasted five hours, as the king's troops were constantly assisted by the passing peasantry, armed with any weapon they could lay hand on, and in those days no Englishman was ever without a bow and sheaf of arrows. Owing to the peculiar nature of the ground, the troops of Audley could not act with sufficient strength; moreover, they had permitted themselves to be taken by surprise.

Lord Audley fell fighting gallantly, together with Sir Thomas

Dutton, Sir John Dunne, Sir Hugh Venables, Sir Richard Molineaux, and Sir John Leigh. His force was completely routed, with the loss of 2,400 men. In this conflict the Cheshire yeomen were the greatest sufferers, as they all wore in that day little silver swans, the Prince of Wales's badge, which the queen had ordered to be distributed among the gentlemen of that county.

At the head of the stream, a stone was afterwards set up to mark where Lord Audley fell in this battle; after winning which, the Earl of Salisbury, having opened a passage for himself by the sword, rushed on to join the Duke of York, who was using troops in Wales, arid safely reached the general rendezvous of the malcontents at Ludlow. To this place the Earl of Warwick brought a body of well-trained English troops from Calais, where they had been serving for some time; but habit and discipline made these men loyal, and, to the utter dismay of the Yorkists, who greatly depended upon them, they marched off in the night, under their leader, Sir Andrew Trollop, and joined King Henry. Every man among the insurgents now mistrusted his neighbour. Blore Heath had been won in vain; for the duke fled to Ireland, Warwick and others to Calais, and their party melted completely away.

ST. ALBANS

The summons to rise again was given in the following year by Guy, Earl of Warwick, Governor of Calais, one of the most remarkable men of his time. His ability in the Cabinet was fully equalled by his intrepidity in the field; he was fertile in expedients, capable of attempting anything, and, from subsequent events, became known to England by the sobriquet of "The King-maker." He landed in Kent, where the people loved him, flocked to his standard, and followed him to London, which he entered amid the acclamations of the populace; and after a conflict at Northampton, Henry became a' second time the captive of the Yorkists under Warwick. Then the crafty and ambitious duke, who had hitherto been struggling for the Protectorship, boldly laid claim to the throne; and Parliament

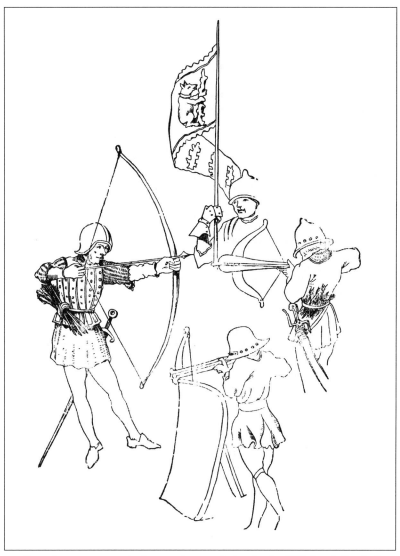

Crossbow-man, pavisaier, archer, and standard of Richard, Earl of Warwick. From a MS. of the 15th century.

actually agreed that after Henry's death the crown should pass to the Duke of York and his heirs.

The maternal heart of Margaret of Anjou resented this foul injustice to her son, the little Prince Edward of Wales; and summoning the Lancastrians to her side in Yorkshire, they routed and slew the duke, whose head, garnished with a crown of paper, was placed on the walls of York. His son, Edward, Earl of March, a brave and handsome youth of nineteen, was heir to his father's claim' and ambition. The hearts of the people inclined to him, and at Mortimer's Cross he swept the royal troops, under the Earl of Pembroke, before him; but amid the snow, on the 17th of February, 1461, there ensued another bloody contest, the second battle of St. Albans, which came about in this manner.

The spirited queen was in the field with an army, on her march to London, when she heard of Pembroke's defeat; but she did not lose heart, conceiving that if she appeared before its walls the citizens would expel the Earl of Warwick, who seemed to have something of the same idea, as he preferred to march forth and fight her in the open country, which doubtless he would not have done had he been quite sure of the populace.

With an army - if indeed it could be called so - consisting of 18,000 men, according to some accounts, a wild and disorderly force, composed of English, Irish, Welsh, and Scots - the latter being some of the broken men of the borders - and all prone to commit the most savage depredations, she had halted at the loftily-situated town of St. Albans, in Hertfordshire, twenty miles north-west of London, where tidings came that Warwick was on his march to attack her, with a force that was small, though increased by a body of Londoners, who had had forfeited all title to the throne when he joined his queen, the young Duke of York was at once proclaimed king, with the title of Edward IV. The animosity between the two factions now become more deadly and implacable. The queen had retired to the North, where, as great multitudes flocked to her standard, she was able in a few weeks to muster 60,000 men, against whom, having now combined their forces, the young king and Warwick advanced with 40,000, in full hope to crush the House of Lancaster for ever, for Edward issued orders that no quarter whatever was to be shown if a battle was won.

In the meantime, Henry and Margaret were at York, and heard with satisfaction that Edward was advancing, as a victorious engagement alone could lead to their restoration. They made the Duke of Somerset general of their army, and waited calmly in York the issue of the battle that was to decide their fate.

TOWTON

On Palm Sunday, the 29th of March, 1461, the two armies came in sight of each other between Saxton and Towton, in the West Riding of Yorkshire, and there ensued, amid a heavy storm of snow, one of the most sanguinary battles ever fought in England.

The land was "merry England "no longer now; it was, says Voltaire, "a bloody theatre, where they were continually erecting scaffolds on the very field of battle." Philip de Comines, in his Memoirs, states that "the custom in England is, when a battle is won, to give quarter, and no man is killed especially of the people, for they know everybody will follow the strongest side, and 'tis but seldom are ransomed. King Edward told me that in all the battles which he had gained, his way was, when the victory was close, to mount on horseback and cry out to 'save the common soldiers, and put the gentry to the sword,' by which means few or none of them escaped." But on this day at Towton there was no such reservation made.

To evince their own resolution, Edward and Warwick,

proclaimed throughout the army "that whoever had a mind to depart, might freely do so before the battle; but when once it was begun, whoever fled should die." Then the earl drew his sword, and kissing the blade, swore that "though the whole army fled, he would die rather than leave the king."

The army of Edward IV advanced in three lines, at nine in the morning. The first was commanded by Lord Falconbridge, in absence of the Duke of Norfolk, who had fallen ill; the second was led by Edward in person, the housings of his horse, which are still preserved in the Tower, being of crimson velvet, powdered with suns and white roses, the badges of his family. On his helmet was the lion of England, and in his hand a long lance with a vamplate of peculiar form. Under his orders was the Earl of Warwick. The third line was led by Sir John Wenlock and Sir John Dynham. As the lines drew near, Edward dismounted, to fight on foot. The snow, which was falling heavily, was drifted by a keen wind right in the faces of the Lancastrians, whose van, led by the Earl of Northumberland, began the battle by a flight of arrows which did no great execution, in consequence of a stratagem used by Falconbridge. The English in war then used two kinds of arrows, one called the flight and the other the sheaf arrow. The former was lightly feathered, with a small head; the latter was high-feathered and shortly shafted, with a large head. As the make of these arrows was different, says Spelman, so was their use. Flight arrows were shot at a great distance, and, at a proper elevation, would kill at two hundred and forty yards. Sheaf arrows were for closer fight, required but a slight elevation, and were often shot point-blank.

Lord Falconbridge ordered his men to let fly a shower of sheaf (not flight) arrows, with a greater elevation than usual, and then to fall back some paces, and halt The Lancastrians perceiving now that the enemy was within range, and supposing that the van had drawn nearer, though still uncertain of their exact distance, by the thickness of the falling snow-flakes, they too let fly a flight of sheaf arrows, which consequently now fell far short, and not only did no mischief to the Yorkists, but, by sticking in the ground with the shafts sloping at an angle towards them, greatly incommoded their own movements as they advanced. The whole ground was studded by these useless arrows, as the Yorkists shot so fast that their quivers were speedily empty. As soon as they were thus half-disarmed, the vanguard closed in upon them, and the wildest havoc began. "It would be difficult," says Rapin, "to describe this terrible battle at large; most of those who have mentioned it, not understanding the art of war, have, instead of representing the several circumstances, given only a confused idea thereof. Besides, the two armies are to be considered as trusting more to their own courage than to the experience of their generals." Even King Henry's order of battle is not recorded.

While the van, under Falconbridge, with their bows slung, fell on the Yorkists with sword, axe, and maul, the next line came on shooting so fast, at an elevation, into the "rearward" of the Yorkists, that after their own arrows were expended they shot those that stuck upward in thousands among the snow. A fearful struggle and butchery-ensued; both armies were alike brave, and both were inspired by the most rancorous hate. For hours the hand-to-hand mêlée raged, without any great advantage being won by either side. The whole plain was covered with corpses, and the blood lay in great pools amid the snow; for ten hours the conflict continued, while the rival armies had become two fighting mobs. Just as night was closing in, the sudden appearance of the Duke of Norfolk, with, a reinforcement to the Yorkists, caused the adherents of Henry to lose all heart, and take to flight; and in the pursuit the nobles, knights, and men-at-arms of Edward, who personally had displayed the most brilliant valour, executed his cruel order to the letter, by giving quarter to none.

In their retreat the Lancastrians rallied more than once, making the slaughter still greater, as they were always compelled to give way; and at last the fugitives fled *en masse* towards the bridge of Tadcaster, but, in despair of reaching it, because they were so closely and fiercely pursued, they turned aside to pass a stream called the Cock, a tributary of the Wharfe. -There, in the hurry and confusion, hundreds fell in the water, and their bodies formed a ghastly bridge for those in the rear. So great was the slaughter there, that even the waters of the Wharfe, far down below that place, were tinged deeply with blood. For three days the slaughter is said to have continued.

According to Stow, Hall, Holinshed, and others, there fell 40,000 men in this battle; and of these, 36,776 were adherents of the deposed King Henry.

Among the dead were Henry, Earl of Northumberland; the Earl of Westmoreland; his son-in-law, Thomas, Lord Dacres, of Gillesland; Lionel, the Lord Welles, K.G.; Sir John Neville;' and Sir Andrew Trollop. Among the prisoners taken were Thomas Courtenay, Earl of Devonshire, and James, Earl of Ormond, who were both beheaded, a fate that fell on many more. Sir John de Ormond, brother of the last-named, also fought at Towton for King Henry, but escaped, and died on a pilgrimage to the Holy Land. The body of the Earl of Northumberland was borne from the field to his own mansion in the Walmgate of York, and was interred there in the Church of St. Denys, where his tomb, denuded of its brasses, is still pointed out.

Margaret, with Henry and the prince their son, now fled for shelter to the King of Scotland, to whose honour it was that he remained aloof; and did not, like the Edwards of other times, take any advantage of the civil strife in England. The 26th of June saw young Edward crowned in London, Henry pronounced an usurper, and his adherents attainted. Edward further confirmed his power by liberally rewarding his friends, and forming such alliances with Scotland and France that the indefatigable Margaret of Anjou, after applying to the Courts of both countries, was unable to procure effective aid from either.

But the Wars of the Roses were not yet ended, even after Henry, when, in 1464, he was captured amid what were then the wilds of Lancashire, was cast as a state prisoner into the Tower of London. But that year saw the star of his rival begin to decline. The young king's marriage with Elizabeth Woodville incensed the haughty Nevilles, of whom king-making Warwick was the head, and this jealousy deepened till it ended in an open quarrel. Warwick, aided by the Duke of Clarence, raised an insurrection among the men of York and Lincoln: but bodies were forced to flee to the Court of Louis XL, where they met Margaret of Anjou, with whom they now made common cause to dethrone Edward IV, and they sought to gather together the broken remains of the Lancastrian party, many of whom were in

The Battle of Townton.

foreign lands, and in such penury that Philip de Comines relates that he himself saw the Dukes of Somerset and Exeter begging their bread from door to door, till their sufferings excited the compassion of Philip, Duke of Burgundy. The new union was further cemented by the marriage of Margaret's son, Prince Edward, to Anne, daughter of Warwick.

CHIPPING BARNET

After an exile of five months, the King-maker suddenly landed at Plymouth, without resistance, on the 13th September, 1470, and the Lancastrians, and many of the ancient nobility, who envied the sudden growth of the house of Woodville, flocked to join him. In one day 6,000 men tore the white roses from their caps, and cried "God bless King Harry VI!" Edward, who had to fly, was denounced as a usurper, and the old king was brought from his cell in the Tower. But this revolution, the effect of the mere giddiness of a faction, was of short duration. No sooner was Warwick at the helm of the State than, without being guilty of one unpopular act, he felt his power begin to decline. Edward was emboldened to return, and, on being supplied with ships, men, and money by the Duke of Burgundy, who had married his sister, he landed at Ravenspur, in Yorkshire; and by the time he reached Nottingham he had under his standard many thousand men who wore the white rose, and 300 Flemings armed with hand-guns.

At Chipping Barnet, in the county of Hertford, on the ground which is still marked by an obelisk, the rival hosts drew near each other in order of battle early on the morning of Easter Sunday, the 14th of April, 1471. The Lancastrian army had encamped the preceding night on Gladmore Heath, a mile north of the little market-town. Edward had under his banner 10,000 men; the Lancastrians were equal in force. Both armies had artillery, but Warwick's was the better served, and as the adverse lines had drawn near each other in the night preceding the action, it played long in the dark on the troops of Edward, but did little or no execution, as all the balls flew over them and fell in the rear, the night being so gloomy and misty that neither leader could clearly see the other's exact position. But with the earliest light of dawn the battle began, between the hours of four and five in the morning.

In Edward's army the first line was led by Richard, Duke of Gloucester, then in his eighteenth year; and it proves the high opinion entertained of his talent and bravery, though this was the first battle in which he "fleshed his maiden sword." The second line was led by Edward himself, together with the Duke of Clarence, whom he had just recovered out of the hands of Warwick; and with this line he placed the helpless and hapless King Henry, "having brought him out of the Tower on purpose to be shot at." William, Lord Hastings, K.G., led the rear or third line. Exclusive of these three lines, Edward had a reserve column, for occasional or special service, and it proved of the greatest use. He on one side, and Warwick on the other, encouraged their troops with all the eloquence of which they were masters; both were as good orators as they were accomplished swordsmen.

In the army of the latter, the right wing was led by John Neville, Marquis of Montague, K.G., and John de Vere, Earl of Oxford; the left wing by Warwick himself, and John Holland, Duke of Exeter. His centre was composed of a body of archers, led by Edmund Beaufort, Duke of Somerset. Where the artillery were posted is left untold.

Having taken up their ground in the dark, Edward's left wing was overlapped or outnumbered by Warwick's right. Seldom has a battle been fought with more obstinacy and bravery than that of Barnet; the personal interests and feelings of all engaged were involved in the issue. Each would be treated as a rebel if the other were victorious; and the barbarous rancour now infused in the war made them all aware that the defeated had no prospect before them but exile or death.

After a few shots exchanged through the rising morning mist, with shouts and yells of defiance, they rushed to engage at close quarters; and very speedily victory seemed to favour Warwick, whose example made all his troops determined to conquer or die. He had detached some squadrons from his third line, under the Earl of Oxford, to attack Edward's left wing, which they assailed with such fury that they broke it, routed and drove it fairly off the field, so that many who had been in its ranks fled as far as London with news that the king was defeated.

Though this event was discouraging, Edward did not lose that presence of mind which is so necessary in a leader. Ordering a body of the reserve, which he kept ready for any special emergency, at once to the front, it fell upon the exposed flank of Warwick, just as the Earl of Oxford was returning with his command to his old ground; and, singular to say, this very movement led eventually to Warwick's defeat. The Earl of Oxford's badge upon his banner, surcoat, and housings was a star, with streamers, and the device of Edward was a sun. The mist which yet lingered about the field prevented Warwick's first line from distinguishing the difference in these heraldic cognisances; so it furiously "charged these squadrons as they were returning to their post, and put them to the rout before the Earl of Oxford had time to remove their mistake."

"Treachery!" was now the cry, and many, on finding themselves attacked by their own men, fled in their bewilderment to the enemy, and were instantly cut down. Others, seeing them running in that direction, thought they were attacked in the rear, and knew not which direction to take, or what to do; so all became confusion. Then Edward, pushing onward at the head of his troops, who were steady and in perfect order, line upon line, fell mercilessly upon the wavering bands of Warwick. On foot, and fighting sword in hand, the latter did all that valour, all that eloquence could do to remedy the mistake, the disorder, and to animate his men, by hewing a passage among the Yorkists where the press was thickest; and perished, covered with wounds, under their bills and spears. Anxious to succour or to save him, his brother, the Marquis of Montague, was slain a few minutes after; and then their forces gave way. As usual, great slaughter followed, for Edward, who was wont to publish before battle generally "that the common soldiers should be spared and the nobles put to the sword, had now ordered that no quarter should be given." The Earl of Oxford and the Duke of Somerset escaped, and the latter went to Wales, where Pembroke was levying troops for Warwick. The earl and some

The obelisk at Chipping Barnet.

of his followers reached St. Michael's Mount, in Cornwall. Disguised as pilgrims, they obtained admission to the castle, and cruelly massacred the whole of the king's garrison.

On the field of Barnet there fell on the king's side the Lords Cromwell and Say, the Lord Montjoy's son, and Sir Humphrey Bourchier. The Duke of Exeter was left for dead on the field, wounded, stripped, and bloody, but crawled to a house close by, whence he found means to reach London, where he obtained shelter in Westminster Abbey.

According to Hall, 10,000 were slain on both sides in this battle; Stow reduces this number to 4,000. All were interred in one common grave on the field, where a mortuary chapel, for anniversary masses, was afterwards erected in memory of them.

The body of the gallant and princely Warwick, and that of his brother, John Neville, Marquis of Montague, who was also a Knight of the Garter, after being exposed to the people for three days in St. Paul's Cathedral, were conveyed to Bisham Abbey, in Berkshire, and there interred. Warwick was in his day unquestionably the greatest and most splendid of the English nobles. "It is said,"says Spelman, "that any soldier might go to his kitchen and take away as much meat as he could carry on the point of his dagger, which is a strong proof of the hospitality of Warwick and the simplicity of the age in which he lived. No less than 30,000 persons are said to have lived at his board in the different manors and castles he possessed in England."

On the afternoon of this memorable Easter Sunday, King Edward went to solemn prayer in St. Paul's Church, to which he presented his royal banner.

The obelisk in memory of the battle was erected in 1740, by Jeremy Sambroke, and the keeper of an inn close by was long wont to exhibit a ball found on the field. It weighed only one pound and a half. The unfortunate Henry was once more replaced in his old prison, the Tower.